# Walking In Wholeness

BY: TRE'ELLE TOLBERT

To my husband, Samuel,

Thank you for being my rock, counselor, my pastor, and support system. Thank you for covering me in prayer, standing guard over my soul, and handling me with care. Thank you for fighting with me and never leaving my side. You are truly a blessing to me and our children. I love you

To my dear children,

SJ, Kristen, Noelle, and Noah,

I would also like to dedicate this book to you all. You all are my lifeline. I have the pleasure to be called mom, and little did you all know, the very existence of your life was the added fuel needed to give me a new strength to fight. The innocent and pure love you guys show, gives me life. It makes me fight for wholeness even more. Thank you all for being patient with me, as I was a bit distant writing my story. I promise it was worth it.

Mommy loves you

*Beloved, I pray that you may prosper in all things and be in health, just as your soul prospers. For I rejoiced greatly when brethren came and testified of the truth that is in you, just as you walk in the truth. I have no greater joy than to hear that my children walk in truth.*

*-III John 3:2-4, NKJV*

*A Letter to You*

Dear Reader,

First and foremost, I'd like to say thank you for purchasing my first book ever! I've held this book near and dear to me because I open up about intimate moments in my life.

These accounts are true and I do not tell them in chronological order. However, I will take you on a journey. Every detail will connect throughout the story.

I wrote this book like a conversation. You will experience some of my Gullah/Geechee dialect within the text.

You will also discover that I pray throughout this text and openly share my faith, my struggles, and how I made it through. I use a bit of science and psychology to paint a picture but you won't be left in the dark. This text is a book of light. It's not designed to bring condemnation but freedom.

As you read this text, you will experience many emotions, but understanding. Hopefully, scales will be removed off of your eyes. I hope that you are awakened to signs, actions, and be made aware of triggers.

This book is written for mature audiences.

# Table of Contents

**Part I**

**Part II**

## Part III

## PT. I

# The Beginning

# Introduction

Walking in Wholeness was a book I never intended to write. I have a story. We all do, and I'm sure we can all agree that our stories are what shapes us into who we are. We can't change who our parents are, we can't change where we grew up, or change the traumas we may have endured throughout life. What we can change is the way we internalize every moment. We can shift our perspective and ways of thinking. We can pull ourselves out of the dark places and move towards the Light.

In this book, I am going to reveal my story. I didn't have the confidence to do so during any other moment of my life. Something happened to me while I was running away to find myself. I ran into God and it was the darkness that pushed me in the right direction.

What I've experienced in my life is something I wish didn't occur because of the pain. And yet it was the greatest blessing because it made me who I am and was the driving force to my becoming. Unfortunately, what I went through happens more often than none, especially in the African American community.

We are taught to be silent. We are taught not to bring shame to the family. To the point, it's an unspoken rule that we all follow. Really, we created a breeding ground to be darkness's playground. Those dark doors remained open from generation to generation and would get stronger and stronger. The innocent ones would become a sacrifice, and no one would speak about it.

Well, I'm going to share with you the past 20 years of my life. I spoke about it in a private place, but now it's time for me to share it with you. You who I may or may not know. You who may or may not identify with the experience but can identify with the roots. You who may have gone through the same thing but were too afraid to speak. I'm here to break the silence. I'm not here to bring shame upon my family but bring glory to the Name of Jesus, who brought me through this. Yes, I'm giving honor to God first! It was only by his love why I'm still standing here with a heart filled with love and in my right mind.

Before I jump into this book and expose my skeletons, let me tell you the moment that led me to share such intimate details about my life.

# My Why

I wrote this book during a time of consecration, which is a place where I had to be separated from all that I once knew. I made a promise to God that I will share with you all the truth because it's in the truth and light where darkness flees. I purposely wrote this book in silence away from the world. Even in plain sight, I was hidden. No phones, limited social media, divine conversations, but most importantly just God. If I were to speak about my book before time, I risk the chances of outside influences trying to tell me how to write my story. I would risk the chances of diminishing its power because I would want to protect the names of those I will discuss in this book.

Truth be told, there is no name to defend other than the name of Jesus, and I trust that he will not put me to shame. If you are reading this book and you are nervous, don't be. I pray that as you read, you will understand that everything that looks great on the outside isn't good. That there are wounds that take place internally that makeup, hair, a banging outfit, and shoes cannot mask. Wounds that multiple degrees, promotions on your jobs, money, clout cannot heal. There will never be true satisfaction of life and freedom if we suppress or hide our story.

For the sake of this book, I vow to be honest, completely open, and transparent because I believe that someone, maybe you, who is reading this would be changed and delivered as you read my story. I am telling you from the most authentic place that this really happened. My traumas manifested in many different ways in my life.

As I am "Walking in Wholeness" I need you all to understand that this is my truth. This is my story. This is what happened and I'm sharing this withholding tears, fighting through tough emotions, so that I can get to the point of sharing with you all how I became free. I want you to be freed after reading this. I pray that this kickstarts your journey to wholeness. I'm not sharing this to bash anyone, or have you feel sorry for me, No. I'm really great! The Lord has really done work for me. The first work was coming to the truth of everything and being delivered. The moment I embraced wholeness, was the where I said yes to be more like God and meant it. My yes was what placed the fire under my tail that was ignited by a prophetic dream I had in July of 2020.

## My Prophetic Dream

I dream of me being in Walmart. I was shopping around with no real purpose. I was wandering in an oversized T-shirt without any undergarments. I was loose, improperly covered to be in public, and no clear reason to be there. I was walking down the main aisle by the checkout area where I saw a well-known apostle of our time. He has the oil and though we've never met officially. He means a lot to me and I knew why the Holy Spirit would choose him because of what and who he represents.

The apostle was near the checkout line where the battery center is and I froze when I saw him. Immediately, I felt this conviction and wanted to hide from him. So, I went in line with no items and no cashiers. I was trying to find a way out when he came from around the other register line to meet me head-on.

We locked eyes. The apostle started clapping his hands and stomping his feet to create a tempo. He took us back to church in the checkout line. While the apostle clapped and stomped, other shoppers in other lines began to join in. The dude was forming a choir in Walmart. Apostle cut on the register light which was number 8 and began singing. I don't remember the sound and tone, but the words were "Demons can't live here".

I was immediately offended. Pride immediately shows up and I denied the song with an attitude. I'm like, "He's not talking to me." I didn't want to believe that he was speaking to me because I know me, and I'm not afflicted. He didn't stop singing. The people kept clapping. It became contagious to the point I started singing it. That's when things began to stir within me. I felt a churning in my body and before I knew it, I was going through deliverance at the checkout counter. When I came to, I was fully clothed in a nice business suit. What a moment!

While I was walking out of the store, I was approached by the apostle again. He would tell me about all that he likes about me. For example, my ability to help fill the need without anyone asking for help. He also shared that I have a way of not letting my environment get to me. He said I knew how to adjust. That's when I shared that it's due to my former career in the Navy.

Then, I looked at him and he looked at me. Eye to eye. My heart breaks and pain would flood my body, while the apostle cries out with tears flowing. He said You've been touched. And he gave me a hug that I could melt in. I don't trust men. I don't care who you are. For him to give me a hug, was for me to feel the

love of God. It was at that moment he grabbed my

shoulder and said, "Write your Book, there are pages in

you. NO word will be wasted." So now, I'm writing it

out. I will pray towards the end of this book, but I pray

NOW that as you read my story, you will be delivered

and free.

# *Chapter 1*

I was assigned to tell my story and to be honest, I don't know how to begin because there is so much to be told. Right now, my husband is sharing in his own book "Loving a Fragile Woman," the past 8 years of our lives, which were the most vital moments to my healing and deliverance. I'd encourage you to read that to hear his perspective of dealing with my traumas and how we survived. Yes, WE! He had to bear my pains as well once I began to open up.

You see the thing about it is, I was young when perversion made a home in my body. It began at the earliest age of 5 years old. I'll share that in a second but let me properly introduce myself to many of you who don't know me. I am Tre'elle. Currently 30 years old, born and raised in Beaufort, South Carolina. I'm Gullah/Geechee and I love my hometown. It's small, quaint, and has its own Lowcountry way of living that you can't experience anywhere else. You may read and hear my dialect come out during this book, so to all those who may read that are not familiar with Geechee, go look it up to gain an understanding.

I was born to really cool parents who were from the area, different cities. Leaving home would be hard when both sides of the family live there but it's something I had to do at the age of 18. I have an older brother and that's it. My mom gave birth to two kids even though she came from a large family of 8. She also has a twin brother. My father also came from a large family of 8. He's kid 6 out of 8.

I was raised on my mom's side the most. I really can't speak much of my dad's side because we didn't deal with them as much. My dad's side of the family is loving and family-driven, but our family wasn't always included in the festivities. To be completely honest, I never felt like I belonged over there after a certain age. My grandparents were nice but that's about it. I never really had the chance to feel their heartbeats only desires and expectations that were somewhat met. Fond memories of laughter, but also memories of being torn apart because of whatever unresolved issues that happened during my parent's marriage.

My grandma on my mom's side is my heartstring. That lady is everything a grandma should be. She cooks, she loves, she chastises, she grows her own food, she feeds the neighborhood, and is the extension of the love that every grandchild desires. I didn't have a grand-father on that side, but she overcompensated for all 40 something of her grandchildren. I don't know my grandfather much. All I know is he has an identical twin brother, he lived across the highway, he has another family and my grandma raised 8 kids as a single parent.

I came from a two-parent home, something my mom never experienced. My father was enlisted in the Marines, and my mom was a hairstylist, and we lived comfortably. My mom made sure my hair was laid and I had to stay clean. She's a very strict lady. I'd think she was the meanest person ever because she never raised my brother and me to be loose. We grew up with man-ners, church every Sunday, good meals, and a lot of rules. As I grew up, I began to understand why my mom would be so hard on us. She never allowed us to sleep over anywhere, I don't care who you were. I could only sleepover at my favorite aunt's house (may she Rest in Peace).

She didn't let me out of her eyesight. She would teach me at the earliest age how to cook, clean, and take care of myself. She taught me as I took a bath, how to detect inappropriate behaviors and to report if someone ever touches me. Stuff that had me confused because I didn't understand any of those gestures. Who's going to touch me? I never said anything nor asked why because you never question an adult. Kids must stay in a child's place. I took heed but I didn't listen. Now that you know this condensed background of me, let me address the moment perversion knocked at my door.

**Perversions Knock**

At the age of 5ish, I had a cousin of mine who was clearly being molested. I didn't know anything about that word or understood the signs then because I wasn't exposed to that type of stuff yet. We were at my grandma's in the bathroom together for some reason together. I remember her touching me in the places my mom said people should never touch. I froze. I didn't know what to do. She tried to show me, but I wouldn't move. She then questions me like do I have a feeling? I'm like, the feeling of what? She said the feeling to hump. I'm looking stupid at this point, like huh?

What feeling? What feeling are you talking about, No, and I ran out the bathroom confused as heck! I told my big brother. He didn't know what else to do so we told our other male cousin who's a complete joke! This dude still to this day cannot be taken seriously. They turned her questions into a song. "Von, you got the feeling? The feeling of what? The feeling to hump?" For those who don't know what hump means, it is having sex with clothes on or off. My cousins would sing that every time they saw me. The song went viral in my family before there was a Facebook. Therefore, I will never forget the memory.

She was embarrassed. I was embarrassed for her. I chose to stay away from her or would avoid her whenever I'm on that side of town. The thing is I never told my mom. I never told her because I was really afraid of her. I thought I would get in trouble because I got in trouble a lot. I was the curious child that would put my hands on the hot stove to see if it was hot. I did that twice actually. I was the one who put aluminum foil in the microwave and made the microwave explode and filled the entire house with smoke, while our parents were out.

I always got my behind cut (a whooping) so this was one time I made up my mind that I wouldn't say anything. One, because I loved my cousin. Two, we were very close, and three, I could ignore it and stay in a child's place. The warning my mom gave me as a kid, as she taught me how to wash, to tell her if anyone touched me to let her know, I didn't do it. I believe it was that moment perversion made a home or planted a seed that would later grow into a castle.

Perversion knew I wouldn't say anything. It knew that I was afraid to tell the people that mattered. I told the wrong people and they made a joke out of it. It knew that it could destroy me. The seed was planted, and I had no idea that staying silent would bite me in my later childhood years. Another naked truth was there was a feeling of pleasure. There was a tingle.

## A Family That's Divided

As we grew up, she never bothered me again. She was embarrassed and the subject was taboo. I started being mean to her. A part of the reason wasn't that she touched me, but my family is divided. My grandma and my great-grandma had sides. They lived next door to one another and yet, I would stay at my grandma's house and very rarely go to my great-grandma's house. There was an invisible line of tension like we didn't belong there as grandkids. Yes, my great-grandma showed favoritism in our eyes. She treated those who she raised better than those she didn't. But let me make one thing clear. I had favor in my great-grandmother's eyes. She always was so proud of me.

Anyways, I would later find out that this was a generational thing that was taboo in our heads because of the stories we heard from our parents. Either or, my cousin who touched me inappropriately was raised by our great-grandma. Our great-grandmother was beautiful and was filled with much wisdom. She sold Jungle Juice boxes and Huggies barrel juices, the big ones not the little ones you get now. During the summer, the grandkids (my grandmother raised) would have to pay while the other great-grand's my grandmother raised could get it for free.

We had to drink from the spicket (water pump), and if we had to use the bathroom in her home, we weren't allowed to use the toilet. We had to use a bucket next to the toilet and dump it outside. Like huh?! You could only dump it if you did the number two too.

So, flies were always around the bucket. I kid you not, we would pee outside first before we used her bathroom. If we used the toilet and flushed it, it was a switch that would come right after. Yes, we'd get chopped.

So, what does that have to do with the way I treated my cousin, mostly everything. We grew up jealous of one another but would put the best foot aside. I remember finding a juice bottle that came from our great-grandma's house. It was orange. I put it in the cup and mixed it with mud juice, so I put the dirty water in the juice and poured it into a coffee cup, and gave it to her to drink. She did and spit it out and we all laughed. Y'all this is some unhealthy behavior.

So, yes, that's what happened. Perversion knocked, and my silence gave it the access to build a home. Tensions and division kept us divided. Jealousy also entered and I would soon find out in 5 years that my life would change for the worst.

# Chapter 2

In between the ages of 5 and ten, I would become the biggest tomboy, clumsily, girly, person ever. I wanted to be like my older brother so badly. He was really cool and could do anything he wanted in my opinion. He skateboarded and played basketball, the typical boy. My only female influencers would be my mom and my family members on my mom's side which was flooded with women. Yet, I lived on my father's family property. So, I lived next to my uncles and aunties but there were only two girls, me and my younger cousin who was too young to really play.

## Getting It from Both Sides

I wasn't the type to play with dolls so, I would try to hang with the boys when I was home. I had this one male cousin who would always try to get me to myself. So, he made up games like hide and seek and mommy and daddy. When we are alone, he would kiss me by the trees. I would fight but I was too small. I remember him dry-humping me when I was over at his house. I remember one time when my brother wasn't around, my cousin placed his body on top of me and tried to do the nasty. He'd make me try to touch his private parts and I'm like what in the world? I believe I touched it too.

I never said a word. Once again, perversion was getting stronger and testing the waters. I froze! Now, the feeling my cousin was talking about was getting stronger but never acted on. Unless it's by someone else. I would later find out that I became a target.

On my mom's side, I would still be getting touched inappropriately by other male cousins. There was one who was older than I was by a long shot. He would try to get to me all the time. I was never left alone with him. If I saw him, I went to another room. Once again, silence. This cousin later moved in with us when my family relocated due to my father's military obligations. I'll share those details in a few.

This soon became a new norm. I knew I had to protect myself but it's only so much a little child could do. I'm sure if my mom is reading this she's going to be upset. She always tried to get me to talk to her, but I never knew how to use my words to tell her. I had a muzzle on my mouth. I also felt that I couldn't trust my mom's emotions. She's the nicest most giving woman you'll ever meet. This lady would give you the shirt off her back. My mom has such a great heart but can be easily misunderstood. I don't know what my mom had gone through and what caused her to be triggered. But from my eyes, I just saw someone who was happy but easily ticked off. To her defense, I was also a child so I didn't understand that my mom couldn't be the superhero every day. My mom had to be a single mom for a lot of my childhood because of my father's duties to the Marine Corps.

My father when he was stationed at home would work long days and sometimes longer nights because of duty. For many of my childhood, my mom was by herself. So, I can understand why my mom would lose patience with us.

During my childhood, he went to Japan twice, deployed in Iraq, and always on call. His career was demanding, and my mom did the best that she could do. She did a great job! Yet, I was still afraid to talk to her about this stuff. I didn't want her to be angry with me. I didn't have an outlet either. I couldn't trust anyone anymore. The closest thing to an outlet for me was church.

## The Church and My Love for Music

I will share my experiences about church throughout this book because the church was a vital part of my childhood. I. As a little kid between 4 to 7, I went to this small white church that had the baddest choir and musicians. This was the first church where I hung around other children my age that weren't my family members. We would play during rehearsals and battle vocally who's better. I loved the church because of the music and the kids. I wish I could say the same about the word, but I was asleep or standing up as a form of punishment because I went to sleep.

My mom is a singer, but she came from a family of singers. My grandma's era had a quartet group back in the day. They sang with known artists of their time like Lee Williams and the Something cavaliers. Either way, my earliest memories of them were coming in the house after playing outside all day during a family reunion and everyone gathering around singing songs like "Slow Train, and It Is Well'.

They were amazing mmk. My grandma and her sisters, my mom, and her sisters would join in and it would sound like heaven. I can also recall my mom and dad battling in the kitchen on their instruments. My dad played the trumpet, and my mom was on the clarinet. She was amazing! We would hear stories about her and my father playing in marching bands together and all that jazz. I was always attracted to music. Music and worship are what saved my life. I'll share how later.

My life was school, home, church. My mom was always singing and being summoned to sing. The church would start at 12 on Sundays and we weren't getting out until 4:30-5 pm. Any additional services were a no-go, my dad wasn't having that (when he was home). My mom was the rebel who wore earrings and I remember her getting preached on across the pulpit because of it.

This was the type of church where we couldn't wear pants, earrings, makeup, but dollies and skirts were welcomed. When that happened, to her, she left. My dad pulled the plug on that one. It was too much control! Remember that word, Control. I would soon find out that control is a monster. I would soon be enslaved to control because of silence and fear.

I had to share with you in the first two chapters my family history and key stories that will lay the foundation for what happens next. How did perversion, church, music, and family play into my life? Let's find out.

*Chapter 3*

The silence I harbored in my heart and mind as a child, allowed perversion to get comfortable. It released a fragrance that attracted other perverse behaviors. I literally became perversion's target! So, let's get to the real reason I shared such intimate but brief details about my family and the reason behind writing this book. At the age of ten, I would be introduced to things that no child in their tiny minds should be introduced too.

### Bullseye

It began when my family relocated to another state due to my dad's orders. Our family had to pack up our single-wide trailer to move to Jacksonville, NC. This was our family's first time moving away from our family. I was nervous but excited. I can't speak for my mom and my brother, but I knew I had high expectations of this move. I was ready to make new friends and see something other than my small town and the crazy behaviors that are there.

Our first home, we lived in the middle of nowhere in Jacksonville. Our neighbors were miles apart and filled with old people. It was a dope house though. I remember being so sad that my brother and I would stare at one another and see who could cry the most. One day, our family members came to visit. It was one of the best moments of our lives. We finally had kids to play with. I remember having to take a bath with a cousin of mine who was the same age as me.

While we were in the bathtub, we started touching each other. I'm sure I started it. I'm sure the learned behavior I experienced caused me to do this. It's such an embarrassing moment for me to share but I was a victim for years and this was the moment I victimized someone else. This was the true moment of hurt people, hurt people, or broken people doing broken things. I internalized this stuff and didn't know it. I knew it was wrong, we both did. It didn't last long. I just remember touching her the way I was being touched and she did the same. It was apparent that we both experienced the same thing and guess what? We never said a word about this moment until I wrote it in this book.

We lived in that home for less than 6 months before moving on base. What a relief! We were surrounded by children our age. I could ride my little black scooter to school. I could walk to the 7-Day store with my older brother to buy Trolli gummies. Play on a basketball court that was right in front of our home. We could go to the movies and bowling alleys.

I made tons of friends. I had a boy crush who I was madly in love with from Miami, Florida. He was my brother's best friend. I even made friends on my own who loved my accent. They said I sounded like I was from Jamaica, I couldn't explain to them Geechee, so I just let them believe what they wanted. With all this fun I, and a place of every kid's dream, this would soon become one of my greatest nightmares to haunt me for the next twenty years of my life.

## The SwimSuit

My mom was a pretty thrifty and frugal lady. She's been shopping at local thrift stores since I can remember. Salvation Army and Goodwill were her time to work with her hands for DIYs, finding vintage clothing, and great finds for her kids. It was an exciting day to come home to new toys and new used clothing that my mom would find for us. It was like hunting for treasure. One of the treasures was this neon and pink two-piece bathing suit my mom found for me. I was so excited to be in two pieces. The thing is when she buys our clothes, she would wash them, and we'll try them on and show her. She'll pump our heads up like, "okay girl! I see you!!"

This was normal for me. One day, when my mom was at church, I tried on that neon swimsuit and I showed my father. There were several other items that I wore, and he said he liked it. Nothing to gas my head up like how my mom would do. When I tried on the neon and pink two-piece and modeled it for my father.

That was the one that got the reaction. A different reaction, but a reaction.

My father grabbed his head and jumped up and hugged me. I'm like yes! This is the winner! I was ten years old. I had my father's approval. I knew I was killing it! He hugged me and didn't let me go. It got weird. But nothing happened. So, I said nothing.

My dad and I started having a lot more time together because my brother was always outside with his friends trying some new skateboard, creating dangerous ramps with pallets and boards they would find, or on another base with his friends at the gym or something. So, I would stay in the house, if I wasn't at work with mom at the hair salon. I had a skateboard but sucked so I'd be off to the side because my brother didn't really have the time to show me. I would try to play basketball, but I sucked at that too and then my mom pulled the plug on me with that because she said she only had one girl and that one girl will not be gay.

So, yes, I was in the house. I didn't have an instrument yet, so I occupied my time with reading. I read a ton of books that were beyond my age level. Needless to say, I was really smart. I also would spend time on our computer so that I could play the Mavis Beacon Typing Institute. I thought it was just a game, but I was learning how to type without looking at the keyboard. I didn't go on the internet much. It was still super slow. I'm showing my age now, but yes, we had dial-up that would disconnect when someone calls the house phone. The computer was in my parent's room.

I'm in the house one day and I don't know many details of what I was doing that day. It was either reading, watching tv, or typing because I didn't have many options. I was in my parent's room where my dad hugged me and told me to give him a kiss. So, I gave him a kiss, but this kiss was on his lips and it was longer than a peck. I don't know how long it lasted but it was very long. So, then he wouldn't let me go. He just kept kissing me and holding me. I'm back in shock! My heart was pounding. My head was spinning. But I froze. He moved me to his bed. I remember him kissing me some more and my stomach was showing. But that's as far as that went. Nothing happened and I didn't say a word.

I was confused now. I don't know what's going on in my life. I didn't want to stay at home anymore. My brother was outside all day or in his room playing with action figures. He was always consumed. When he was outside, I knew I wasn't safe. I would ask my mom to go with her to the salon, but she would say she'll be staying late, and she had church to go to, so it's better to stay home. I would semi beg to be around her now, but work and church were my mom's life. She was busy all the time. Her clientele was at its peak. I would go with her on the weekends (Friday after school and Saturday) but throughout the week if my dad wasn't on duty and we were home from school, I was at the house.

Things started getting worse. My dad started to request every so often for me to be in this neon bathing suit. He would always give me the same reaction as the first time he saw me. I loved that attention the first time but would soon hate it. But I would smile because it made him happy. He began touching on undeveloped areas like my chest and hands would go up and down my premature waste. Kisses began to be no more. I began touching his private parts. Parts that were bigger than the ones I touched as a younger child. We went from touches to strokes. From strokes to head. From head to rockets. Rockets were the game. Rockets were making my father cum and it would be explosive, so it was like rockets launching.

This would be my life for the next 3 years and guess what. I said nothing. In one of those years, I recall one day lying to my mom because my father told me to do so. He told me to tell my mom that I didn't have any school that day. She didn't question me, because I wasn't a liar. Though I was because I was holding a secret that made me a liar every time I held the secret. My mom left and drove past my school on her way to work. Only to see all the bikes and cars at the school. She did question me, but I held on to my lie.

That was the day I'd be "played with" the most... well, until my brother came home. It got to the point where I was had no feelings anymore. I was numb. I masked how I felt and kept it moving. I continued to present to my parents the girl they knew me to be. The smart little innocent child that listens well and stays out of the way. But I didn't know how to cope. I felt guilty looking at my mom. I felt sick to my stomach. I was in a storm. I was in a tempest. (Cues the orchestra to play "The Tempest by Robert Smith). I was losing my marbles. I deserved an Oscar because I guess I hid and masked my pain well.

# Here We Go Again

If things couldn't get any worse, my older male cousin had to leave Beaufort. He did something and needed a place to cool off for a bit. So, my aunt and mom agreed that he'd move up there with us until the heat left. I don't know what he did. I just knew what he did to me while he was there. This was the same cousin that I would avoid when I was in South Carolina. The older one was stronger than me. Here we go again.

He came during the summer to watch my brother and me because mommy and daddy had to work, and we were still too young to be in the house on our own. My brother is 3.5 years older than I am, so I'm about age 11 maybe, so my brother was about

14ish. My older cousin was about 17-18 then. I don't know but the point is he is way older than me.

If I don't go to work with my mom, I'll be home. While I'm at home, my brother and my cousin would be outside playing and doing who knows what. There were moments where my brother would be outside, my cousin would leave him out there to bother me. His room was the converted screen-in porch, as well as, the den. He stayed on the pullout couch. So, while I would be on the couch watching tv, he'd be like you're in my room. So, he would make me lay down on the couch and take my bottoms off. He would whip out his little meat and try to have sex with me. I was never penetrated though. His "vienna sausage" could never stay up. It was always too squishy and couldn't go anywhere.

He would get mad and just stop and tell me to get out. This happened on several occasions. I went to my dad one day and asked him if I was pregnant. He said what?! What makes you think that you are pregnant? I said I don't know. I just think I'm pregnant. The next day, we were taking a trip to Beaufort, and my cousin was gone. I'm not sure if my mom knew this or not but my dad wasn't having it. Of course, my brother was sad, I was happy but not happy. While my cousin was there, I wasn't being bothered by my dad.

## Selling Myself

My numbness got the best of me. It got to the point, I began selling myself for things that I wanted. For some reason, things weren't going well in our household. I remember hearing arguments in my room that my mom and dad would have. They were complaining about the single-wide we moved out of and the lack of payments is causing us to live uncomfortably. My mom's clientele began to decrease for whatever reason. She left a salon to work at another salon. This happened about 2 times while we lived in NC.

I remember seeing my mom crying on the bed surrounded by a lot of pennies. She would be counting them so that my brother and I could eat. We ate at McDonald's once a day off of the dollar menu. My mom wasn't in a good place. We started going to the Salvation Army not because we wanted to but because we had to. Things were really going downhill fast. This is when my molestation would take a turn for the worst. In order for me to get things, I would have to exchange them for rockets. To the point, rockets were a form of payment for me. If I wanted something, I would have to do something in return. I started using it to buy food for me and my brother. It became a form of control.

I would try to repay my debt until I couldn't go anymore but the rockets started having a delay in its launch. There would be a withholding so it could last longer and use that as a way to never allow me to pay it off. I would be angry because I hated it so much. This wasn't fair!

I felt like I was going to die. Truth be told, I was already dead. I would sell myself for the things that I loved the most. I can remember desperately wanting a karaoke machine that had a tv on it and exchanging rockets as currency. I sold myself for the dollar menus at Wendy's because my brother and I were hungry. I sold myself for a snare drum because I wanted to be like Nick Cannon in the movie "Drumline." Everything that brought my soul pleasure, cost my soul so much pain.

Mommy was working, daddy was home on the weekends. He always worked on cars to keep him busy. He would play with us and teach us things like how to drive an automatic and 5-speed car. He would wrestle with my brother and me and still be dad, but dad had a dark side. In the same breath of him teaching me how to drive, I would be alone with him. I would have to be on his lap. I would go to places that were desolate with zero traffic just to give him more rockets or to bring him pleasure.

I never wanted to be alone with him. If we were, I'd be speaking to the spirit of lust. He'd be talking about women and how bad (nice looking) they are.

He'd talk to me about gaps, and how to size a woman up. I would tell him I'm not my brother, but he didn't care. I wasn't speaking to my dad anymore. I was speaking to the broken pieces of him that gave the spirits a voice. We were homies because I could keep quiet. I know this now because while things were happening to me, I would only see darkness. I no longer saw my father. I saw something beyond him. I didn't have the language to articulate that either. How do you communicate this to any sane person without causing harm upon the person you love.

At this time, I was also experiencing high levels of horniness now. I wanted to be pleased and burst through the urges I was having. I would try to not think about it but it wouldn't go away. I'd try to touch myself but it was a huge no for me. The only way I could have relief is to wait for my father or my brother.

## My Brother

My brother was in middle or high school when he began to do the same things that my father did to me. We engaged in lustful activities with our clothes on. I would rub on areas that were off-limits with my hands. We'd kiss. I guess you can say, I learned a lot from my dad. I knew what to do for him to make him happy. I began to develop a sense of satisfaction to cope with my crazy. I would say to myself, I can make them happy, I could save the day. I could be the bridge to keep my parents married because if I tell, they'd get divorced and I'd have an unpredictable future that could be way worse than this.

There was the satisfaction of being a hero to save the day and that's the most perverted thing I'll confess. I'd be the sacrifice is what that meant. I'll be the one to hold this, so that life as we all knew it as a family from the outside looking in could be "normal." This birthed the people-pleaser in me. Going above and beyond to make people stay or so that I am never forgotten.

To make you stay, I just have to give you all of me. My time, my body, my sanity! All I must do is sell myself. Let you touch me, let you get satisfaction, as long as you were satisfied, I was happy that I could do something to make you happy even at the cost of me losing my mind. Even though I hated it, I couldn't stop it. It had become my norm. I have officially normalized dysfunction. I have officially normalized dysfunction.

## Almost Losing My Virginity

One day, I made up in my mind that I was going to have sex for real. I was hanging around some fast girls who were talking about losing their virginity. How it hurt and how great it felt. I was seen as the little innocent child, so they would say things like, "Girl you're cute and you have a body so, when are you going to do it?" I would smile and say nothing. My smile was really a way to hide my pains, like girls if you only knew what I was going through, I'd show you how to do something.

I was never penetrated though, so what's the worst that could happen right. We devised a plan and I would have to lie and tell my parents that I was staying after school for a project so that I could lose my "virginity," even though my purity was gone a long time ago. That day, my mom came to school and disenrolled

me. We were moving back to South Carolina. My mom

was leaving my dad to finish out his obligations in NC.

We couldn't be sustained in Jacksonville anymore.

I didn't get a chance to say goodbye to my

friends, nor teachers. I was loved at that school too.

Once again, coping with crazy was to stay in the books.

I had risen above and beyond as a stellar student who

had the chance to cut the ribbon for the new middle

school. I was the teacher's favorite pupil. I guess all

those books paid off at the cost of me wanting to con-

trol one aspect of my life that is up to me. My intelli-

gence.

# Chapter 4

Moving back to South Carolina, my mom and I lived in the projects with my aunt and her four daughters. My dad was finishing up his tour in NC and My brother was living with our grandma. My family was divided. I was torn with so many emotions and I didn't know how to function. I was out of school for about a month until my mom could get situated to work again. I used my grandma's address to go to school near her home because the project we lived in was way across town and that wasn't the place to go to school and have to wait until my mom got off. So, I would be with my grandma until the end of the night. This was fun so don't be saddened by that moment.

In middle school, I was very advanced and I mean that in every way. I was on the yellow hall, so I had all the smart classes. I was the first chair in band class on my clarinet. I was my director's favorite, but this could be my opinion. I would be used to tune the band class. Tre'elle, give me a concert C. I had a solo during graduation, and so yes, I believed my director saw promise in me.

With all the great things that could make my teachers and parents proud of me, I was still troubled, but no one would have ever noticed. I was a straight-A student and knew how to be a good pupil. I knew how to play my role. All I needed was a script to keep up with my robotic nature. I knew how to satisfy my teacher's expectations of me that were high. I knew how to be the daughter to my mom. I knew how to sat-isfy men, I knew how to make my friends happy, but I was like a zombie. Dead and insensitive to pain and raging in emotions.

## My Inner Struggles with my Mom

In the 8th grade was where things got interesting. My dad would come home to visit us and help my mom start her new salon. This time she was on her own. No booth rent but the boss. Things were finally looking up for her. For me, as I mentioned before, my dad still found the time to take me on the backroads for me to learn how to drive but before I could take the wheel, well, y'all know how this goes by now. If I wanted anything, I had to do something.

My relationship with my mom was also rocky from an emotional perspective. I began to feel hate in my heart because she didn't know what was going on with me because couldn't come out and say it. I tried to give her hints but I hated that missed the signs of me trying to tell her. I wanted my mom to read my mind, hear my heart. The little understanding I had about God, I would cry out to him and ask Him to reveal a sign to her.

There was one particular moment, I felt like my mom couldn't stand me at one point in time. In her eyes, I'm sure everything was perfect, but for me, I felt that she would say some mean and hurtful things to me like I was her punching bag for emotions. Mommy, if you are reading this, I do apologize for the knot you may feel in your stomach right now. This maybe a hard pill to swallow, however, this is my truth. I felt like my brother was her favorite child. He could do anything he wanted and get whatever but I was always struggling for her attention and belonging.

We had nothing in common but singing and hair. I learned how to do hair because she made me. I was never interested in it to be honest because I was forced to do something that I didn't want to do. It was a harmless gesture for me to do hair, but it wasn't my thing. I had no passion or desire to work in a salon. Granted, I'm glad I learned because I have two daughters now, but I didn't like hair but if it kept me away from home then fine. My mom never came into my world. She never really understood me. She knows me but she didn't know me. She didn't know the intimate parts of me, I wanted to be loved. But by that time, I didn't know what that was anymore. I was a troubled teenager now. I didn't know how to think for myself, I only knew how to serve and present a shell that could get me through the next day.

I became a projection of what others saw in me. If I could make you happy then that's what I'll do. If my teachers liked me because I was smart, then let me get smarter, if my mom deals with me because I can talk about hair and music, then so be it. If my dad likes me because he can touch me any way fine. If my brother wants to grab and squeeze me and have sex without penetration then so be it. I wanted to give up but something wouldn't let me. I had to find my way through this. I was melting and no one could see me.

# *Chapter 5*

Moving out of the projects came at the cost of seeing my auntie getting abused by her ex-boyfriend. I've suffered sexual abuse but I've never a man put his hands on a woman, like how my auntie's boyfriend did. My mom jumped in to help her and that was a wrap. My dad came down from NC and purchased our new home.

We lived on the base for a while and My mom was happy. So were me and my brother. We left the projects and now my family is back together. I transferred to middle school (Though I was kicked out but that's another story for another day) and was finally stable. Daddy came home from North Carolina, and I had my family again. Life was great from the outside looking in.

From the inside looking out, I was broken. I was overweight now, bigger than all of my siblings, overdeveloped and underdeveloped at the same time. I was getting teased by my family that I was fat. I felt ugly and unattractive. I was still being molested. I didn't understand life. Moving our home off of base was the icing on the cake with the cherry on top with my relationship with me and my father. We would clear the land to our new residence near his family again. We were literally down the street from my father's parents grandparents. My dad and I would clear the land, but of course I would have to be an extra hand if you catch my drift.

One night, after a long day of working with tractors and pulling roots from the soil, I drove to the gas station to bring back some water for my father and myself. We were technically done with clearing the property. I remember because that was the night, I made up in my mind that my dad could have my virginity. He didn't want to but by this time I'm 13 or 14.

*Before you ask, yes, I could drive to the gas station, remember I could drive for a while now, and I was very mature looking at that time.*

The feeling my cousin was talking about when I was five was strong now. I started craving it and didn't care who it came from anymore. I had to quench this lust. I needed a pressure that I couldn't fill.

When I got back from the gas station, it was dark. I was in the car and I tried to sit on it. He told me to relax and it hurt too bad and he couldn't do it. Something clicked where he couldn't do it. So, we stopped and I felt rejected. I knew I could probably try it again, but something happened that day. I prayed hard because that thought wasn't right and I got sick thinking about it. I prayed that God would take my father away, not to kill him but take him away so that this could end. I didn't want these feelings anymore. I didn't want to be dirty anymore. I didn't want to keep the lies in anymore. I didn't want to live in an alternate reality to cope anymore. I didn't want to see the bright side of things anymore. I wanted the truth. I wanted to be seen for real.

My prayers were answered. My dad would soon deploy again to fight the war in Iraq. I was saved. I could be "normal." Yet, we all know that this was never really my narrative. This was too good to be true.

I wanted to believe that when my father left, so did the molestation, but that's when my brother would come into the room in the middle of the night to come and try to have a midnight snack. The dry sex in North Carolina wasn't working anymore. I would clinch and act like I was still asleep. He would leave and come back. This is what caused me to be a light sleeper. I would hear my door open and I would panic and pray. Like no, no, nooo. This happened for a while, I said nothing and acted as nothing happened.

I remember having sex with my brother as I had with my dad. I didn't like it but liked the feelings of pleasure. I wanted him to take my virginity because there's only so much foreplay could do. I honestly believe there were moments where I began to initiate the touches. He was glued to his ps2 playing Grand Theft Auto or NBA 2K something, but I would watch and we would do what we do. I would even try to pray after like

I'm so dirty. I won't do it again. I liked the feeling, just not who it was from. I knew it was wrong on so many levels.

Honestly, I had a whole inside of me. I began to cry out to God why have you forsaken me? Really, it was more like God where are you? This can't be life! I was angry, I was sad, I was guilty, I was controlled, I was learning how to control, and no one could see me.

# Chapter 6

*"Where was the church"*

I began to despise the church. I wondered why no one could see me. Why can't I tell my mom? It went beyond fear it was something else there. But the church is where God is so I'm going to go because apparently, He didn't see me in my home. The churches I went to still had great music and singing, the word was even better but I wasn't growing. I wasn't seen by the power that I saw causing others to cry. I wanted God, but this wasn't it. I didn't understand it at first like how I do now. But I saw things in church that happened that I didn't reflect my Father in Heaven. I couldn't find God in church. I thought he abandoned me too.

There were revivals after revivals, and yet no change in me. The only thing I loved was the music, to be honest. The Bible I owned was the KJV that the Mormons brought to my house when I was about 8 years old. I could read but I wasn't really feeling the thee's and the thou's. No pastor spoke a language that I could accept. I wanted to understand it. But the only way I could feel God was in my world that I created in mind.

I would have conversations with Christ but I didn't think he was listening. I never got the response I saw in the Bible cartoons with the deep voice and white Jesus that would speak like Mufasa in Lion King. Truth is, I thought I was going crazy but hope in God made me want to believe that I wasn't.

The church wasn't my home. I didn't fit in there. It was too creative and it wasn't accepted. I was never accepted. I always had to do things to fit in. My family members were dancers but I was stiff. They would double Dutch but I couldn't turn the rope because I was double-handed. I knew I could do all those things but I wasn't able to do it because I never had the chance. I never had a chance to really express my creativity in the church. I could sing but too young to sing on the praise team and the children's choir didn't last long. I loved to do visuals but the church already had their software for their little programs. What can I do?

With nowhere else to turn, I turned to God in music. I started playing my clarinet from a deeper place than sheet music. I had a keyboard now, so I began to teach myself how to play my favorite gospel songs. I would lock myself in my room and lay near my boom box in tears crying silent tears of anger, rage, but hope that this can't be my end. I would listen to songs by Donald Lawerence, "The Blessings of Abraham, the Prayer of Jabez, the entire Finale pt. 1 and 2, Karen Clark, "God is here," the songs were very intimate. "Peace Be Still and Oil of God" by Vanessa Bell Armstrong and "Come in the House by John P. Kee, were my jam! Those songs that made my heart cry. I would have my playlist on repeat and I would sing it to the depths of my soul. Music became my saving grace.

I found a new way to cope with pain. It was through music where I had conversations with God. I didn't know it at the time but my room became my secret place. I locked myself in the room and would play and cry and write and scream and do it all over again.

God took me to a place of sanity when I played my sound.

I started hearing new sounds. So I'd request new instruments. This time I didn't go to my father, I went to my band director. I couldn't take the instruments home but I could play with them after school, or I could join a marching band, or I could do things to keep me busy, but I also received a software called Finale Notepad that allowed me to play every instrument from the computer by inputting notes. I was about to become the greatest composer.

Music was the vehicle that kept me in the presence of God. I loved to sing, write, and play the sounds of my heart that were inspired by the sounds I've learned in band and gospel music. If I couldn't get a good word, I knew that I could play a song over and over and hear a different word each time. I didn't know those moments would prepare me for what I'm doing now. I still sing, I still write, and I've added to my vocabulary of instrumentation. I've picked up the guitar now, which is my favorite of them all. But those moments in my childhood taught me that music is just as important.

Church magnified only the word of God, but not the worship of God through music, or dance, or whatever your creative expression could be. Could it be, I didn't feel accepted because I was a creative trapped by religion or traditional ways of thinking that would limit God to only the 66 books? This is no shade to any denomination, but I'd encourage you to seek God to gain your own understanding. He speaks to you in your language. He said my sheep knows and hears my voice.

I couldn't hear him because my language was creativity.

Not form or fashion. Hm.

# Chapter 7

*"Rebellion"*

So far, you've heard about a lot of my traumas as a kid, but I never really highlighted my middle school years. That's because those were the worst. I was in an awkward stage in life. I really didn't understand who I am or what I was to be. The best thing in my life was school and church because that was a script that I knew I could follow. Anything that wasn't school or church I was completely clueless. I didn't have an identity. I didn't know what to define myself as. I was smart, kind, loving, and fat. This was the time I was overweight. I was chunky and I ate a lot. I had to eat what was set before me. I would have super large portions and was not allowed to waste any food.

In my identity crisis, my older slimmer brother would call me out in my insecurities. I was getting called fat all the time with my family members. I got teased, but the thing is they didn't call it teasing or bullying, I was just getting checked about everything.

"Von, you've gained weight " I heard that every day. When my mom would get angry at me, she would say things like look at you, you ol' fat self you ol' worm eye. Y'all, I couldn't take it. I was fat. I was a size 14 in the 8th grade. I couldn't play outside, and I couldn't play sports. I was in the house eating, sleeping, reading, playing an instrument, or now playing the sims. I kept myself occupied, I knew how to stay out of the way and not be seen. I wanted to sneak food because I didn't want to be called out for eating too much. When we would go to buffets, I would try to eat a salad and my brother would say things like *"you know you don't want a salad, you know you want a roll. Why are you acting like that? You betta eat you know you gon' be hungry."* I'd lie and say no but truth be told I would leave Golden Corral hungry. I would take a few rolls though because that honey butter spread was addicting.

I couldn't find myself anywhere. Not in a movie, magazine, doll, nothing but music and being alone. I would stare in the mirror and squeeze my gut. I would compare myself to my cousins all the time. I had one cousin whose looks I'd covet. The same one who asked me if I had the feeling. She was getting all the attention from boys in middle school. Every boy I liked, she got. She was cute, flat stomach and a little booty.

I was cute for a big girl. I was chunky but had a donk. I still had a stained tooth. But I felt inside so ugly. Ugly things happened to me and truth is I probably wasn't that bad, but my outer was only a reflection of my insides. I remember shopping in my mom's closet for clothes. I had a favorite jean, I had big boobies, I was nearly 180 pounds and I was now being compared to an adult (my mom). She did tell me I'd lose the weight, that it was baby weight that I'll drop.

She was somewhat correct. I did lose the weight but not on the account that I had gotten taller and magically dropped the weight. No, I had to wake up early in the morning to go PT with my father who was still in the Marines. I had to get up at 0530 while the house was silent to go with my daddy and run miles around base. I was so slow, I was going to die. I couldn't do it but my dad did encourage me. We'd sing military cadences to keep my mind off the fact that I was fat, sloppy and unattractive. I would sweat my hair out and throw it in one ponytail for school.

I started shedding a few pounds, but I needed to develop a healthy diet. So, I started watching the Food Network to find new ways to cook food that is outside of our culture. I got tired of greens and rice, Lima beans with smoked neck bones and hammocks, food with waste grease in it, I wanted to distance myself from all of that. I started by replacing rice with oatmeal. It was a start. I was developing a healthy habit but I was still losing it because I wasn't losing weight fast enough.

**Truth be told, I had to become a rebel to the control in my home. I had to rebel to gain my healing.**

One day when my dad was in Iraq, I sent him an email saying how I was fat and overweight and getting teased about it. I knew this had to hurt his feelings. He did his best to make sure I felt beautiful by calling me pretty. Can you see why I was unstable? I had to understand and sort the actions of my father from the actions of his afflictions. I can share this later but I knew when I told him I was getting teased, he had to find a solution. He told me to find a sport to join and stay to stay after school. This sport was basketball. Marching band season was over and JV basketball didn't have tryouts. If you came out you made the team because the coach said you will cut yourself. So, that 10th Grade year I changed. I changed for the better. I rebelled against my mom who said I couldn't stay after school. If she had a problem with it, I could just pull the "Well, Daddy said yes," card.

I knew absolutely nothing about basketball. The memories I did have was trying to play by myself when no one else was watching and missing every shot. I sucked so bad. I knew I could do it, once again, I just needed someone to take the time to show me. If you can get me to the level of understanding, I got it. You won't have to show me again. I would pursue it with all of me because I had to prove to myself that I'm not a failure.

I set high goals that's why I was so smart because I wanted to be the best. Basketball was no different. I may be the worst right now, but I will make varsity, I will be a three-point shooter, I will lose weight, I will be confident. This was the reason. I had to gain some type of confidence in something.

In the 10th grade, my brother moved out of the house because he had graduated. So, it was me and my parents. I was like the only child. When my dad had gotten back from Iraq he would meet a different little girl. He would meet a girl who was driven and dedicated to looking different. When he gave me the permission to play basketball, he didn't know that this would be the moment to show me the importance of a team and community. He didn't know that I would become one of the most improved players. He didn't know I would gain confidence. He didn't know that by playing this sport I would reject him. When he made the gestures that he would use to get me to do things, I told him no. I meant it.

Something was happening to me. IT didn't come from the church, it didn't come from being seen by man, but it was because of God, music, and a sport. Truth is  Music saved my life. I didn't know at the time that me playing and praying fervently that God was responding. I didn't know that staying after school for basketball meant that I would develop new friendships, that I would have accountability to keep me busy in a healthy way.

I had games, practice, I was growing up. This was the first time I was happy.  My brother was gone, my father wasn't being used anymore, my mom and my relationship grew but it was because I started to grow up. Oh, and your girl started looking good. I went from 180 something to 160. I was getting snatched and it was like it happened overnight, but it didn't'. This wasn't the baby weight that was dropping. I was dropping the negative thoughts and images of myself. This was the moment of me finding me.

I vowed to myself, in order to make it out of this house, I needed to stay busy. I joined every club, participated in a sport a season, and had gotten a job working part-time to stay away from the house. I joined a choir as well alongside my mom. I couldn't stay away from music. From 10th to 12th grade, I had a car, I had to have a job to pay the insurance and keep gas in it, I would stay after school for marching band, basketball, and track, and from 5 to 10 pm, work at Bruster's Real Ice Cream. The only thing that changed was my job between my high school years. But those next three years was me gaining responsibility, learning how to move throughout life, and become independent.

# Leaving Home

My 12th-grade year in high school was more than a graduation from completing 12 years but a graduation that I survived my traumas. I graduated in the top ten of my class. I was the student body president. I gave a speech during graduation. My face was all over the yearbook. So, I left high school on a high note.

I didn't know that my confidence and drive was the recipe for success because I was accepted into many colleges, full rides to play my clarinet in marching bands, but I knew I had to leave home. I wanted to get as far away from Beaufort, SC as I can and college wasn't enough. I listened to my parents and enrolled in my first year during the summer. I tested out of my freshman year at Columbia College ( the school I picked because of the influence to stay close to home).

That summer I chose my roommates and classes. I went to the college and felt that this wasn't it for me. I felt in my gut that I would get stuck. So, when I came back home from my campus tour with my parents, I started moving incognito.

I went to see a Navy recruiter who had given me his card one day during my senior year of high school. I knew this was the move because of the dreams that I've been having. Once the instruction was vivid, I made my move. I went to MEPS without my parents knowing. When I had gotten back from Ft. Jackson, and I was officially sworn in, I told my parents. My mom cried, my dad was excited for me. This was the beginning of me finding me. This was the beginning of me losing the grips of control that my parents had on me. I didn't know that the control would somehow still exist. It wasn't in the physical anymore, all that I've endured became a spiritual stronghold. My soul was still tied to home and a physical move wasn't enough.

At the ages of 18 to 29.5, I would soon learn that the weapons of warfare are not carnal but that they were spiritual. I would soon find out that I was toxic and perverted in my thinking. I was being controlled by demonic forces and influences by the people who were supposed to have guided me. I would have to face the toughest fight for my life. Enlisting in the US Navy was one thing, but as I fought for the nation's freedom, the biggest war was for me to reclaim the freedom in my mind, body, and spirit.

# PT. II

*The Next Decade*

*Introduction*

The next decade of my life was the darkest time of my life. I didn't know I was carrying such a dark presence around me. The darkness of lies and secrets followed me. It kept me imprisoned. I was in the cave. This was an adult-sized stronghold. My real identity was locked away the moment perversion entered. The real power and authority of me were still in the cave with three ponytails and barrettes. I had to come to the realization that what I experienced in my childhood was not normal. That there were traumas and grenades (triggers) that would cause me to explode. I discovered that I had an odor that attracted the same demons that were sown in me.

I found that I would surround myself with things that were familiar because I became comfortable in my dysfunction. I discovered that I didn't have any discernment and was set up in my time in the military. I would soon find out that my worst fear would come to pass by getting raped at 21 by a friend who had the same symptoms as the two most important men in my life and never tell the right people. Something I picked up at age 5 came back to bite me.

I would have to fight a fight without throwing these hands of mine, but I would have to engage in psychological warfare and my past was a ticking time bomb waiting for me to explode. In the next decade, I will open up about my military life, marriage, and life with children dealing with all my baggage. I will also share with you the revealing of my 20-year secret, unhealthy habits that needed to be broken, how I obtained

my healing, and why I'm "Walking in Wholeness.

# Chapter 8

My life in the military was grand. There were great highs and ultimate lows that placed me at rock bottom in my life. I found myself maturing into adulthood without having an idea of what the real world was like. I was 19-years-old by the time I made it to my first command on the ship. I was a freshman of course, literally fresh out of water. I was surrounded by people who came from all over the world, different backgrounds, and stories.

During my time on the ship, I found myself surrounded by a lot of different cultures and beliefs. I'm from a small town and my mind was closed. I wasn't exposed to much according to my surroundings. Beaufort wasn't a place for children but more of a place for retirees to enjoy the quaint southern charm of the Lowcountry. The church would preach the love of God but they would also preach to be in the world but not of it. I always told, "*If it walks like a duck, quack like a duck, it's a duck*. So, I wasn't really prepared for the influx of freedom of choices until I made it to the military.

## My Gay Best Friend

When I settled in at my command, I remember being surrounded by a lot of homosexuals, and my heart posture towards them was to stay away from me. I also didn't want to be guilty by association. I fought hard for the broken image that I portrayed. I didn't need any additional rejection or hurt in my life by being called something that I'm not.

Something changed the moment I met my best friend on the ship. She was our newest addition to my shop. She was beautiful, black, and smarter than I was. I loved her! But our story was rough. When I found out that another black female was coming to my shop, I was excited. I was the only girl in the shop, so I was really happy that I'd be getting a female. My LPO (leading petty officer) told me to reach out to her and put me in charge of her arrival. Facebook was a thing now, so I found her on Facebook, sent her a friend request and found out that she was gay.

I treated that moment like it was the end of the world for me. I began to be very judgmental but I fossilized the issue in my heart and put on my performance cap. When we finally met, we didn't speak much. I only spoke to her if it was absolutely necessary. She was non-existent because we lived in different worlds. It wasn't until deployment where we were forced to merge our worlds. I finally spoke to her while we were standing watch. We were leaving for a 10.5month deployment and we had to sit next to one another for 5 hours in the engine room. As embarrassing as it is to say, this was the first time I actually had the opportunity to break the ice and speak to her. We had nothing but time. This is when I spoke to her heart not my fossilized judgement and I was wrong. I was soo wrong.

I'm sharing this story because I was filled with so much good and evil. How dare I judge someone who I didn't know without looking at my self-righteousness? I was the example of the Christians you should hate, but that's because I was confused and conflicted. No one taught me about the heart of God, the inner places that desired purity. That's what I found in my friend. She was one of the greatest people I've ever met in my entire life. She was pivotal to my growth because she destroyed my snobbish ways. She told me about myself and my behavior UNFILTERED. It took her to take me outside my comfort zone to deal with my homophobia but it was greater than that. I had to deal with my darkness. She was a mirror for me to look at me first before I fix my heart to say anything else about someone else.

My friends on the ship respected me, many of them were aware of my journey, they knew I love God and I guess I had this light. Many of my friends were not Christians either. There weren't many around on the ship that I could identify with and the ones who had any stench from my hometown, I wanted nothing to do with. I hung around the sinners like myself. My best friend was gay and I was a big fornicating, people-

pleasing person, so I found nothing wrong with in-
dulging in the hearts of people vs the conditions of
people. My homies knew I wasn't about that life and no
one asked me to engage in any activity whether that was
smoking, drinking, anything. If I did it, it was because I
wanted to do so.

## I Grew Numb

However, there was this one moment when I
was on deployment where our ship pulled in port and I
had the idea to try "it" out. What would it be like to kiss
a girl? At this point, I wanted to feel something because
I lost. I was. This feeling of numbness occurred after I
had gotten raped by my friend, whom I adored. I share
this story in a later chapter, but the point is after I got
raped I told God I didn't care what happens to me
anymore.

So the next port visit, the thought of being with another woman came into my mind while I'm in Oman. After sightseeing all day, that night, I found myself at the hotel where they had a bar on the beach. While I was there, I indulged in a lot of mixed drinks. One Marine bought me a bottle of Rose, another bought me a long island, and I began drinking everything that was presented before me.

I was really drunk now. I was having a great time but the more I was drinking the darker I became. The past was starting to haunt me. I tried to drink my pains and sorrows away. I wanted to feel pain because I didn't have any soul anymore. Many on the ship had their companions (we called them "Boat Boo's), I didn't have one. I had many who were interested but not interested in me, just my body. I was in pain because I'm still internalizing the treachery from my homeboy who got the best of me in Palma. The pain was my reminder that I was alive but also a reminder that I wanted to die.

When the thought came to my mind of kissing a girl, I played ping pong with it. I knew how to look at a woman and size her up. My father taught me well as a child how to look and lust. What's the worst that could happen? I remember, I was at the bar and I saw my homegirl. I looked at her and then I "looked" at her being completely vulnerable to the moment that scared the living daylights out of me. I saw something that I've never seen before but was familiar with. I saw this darkness and I got up and walked away, maybe I had one too many Long Islands. I found myself on the outside of the bathroom sitting on this bench. Alone.

When I went to the bathroom, I ran in and threw up. My best friend was in the bathroom as well. She told me that I wasn't being classy and told me to have my pinky up while I'm throwing up my life in a black plastic bag. I saw my homegirl, the one from the bar that I "looked" at, and confessed to her that I wanted to kiss a girl. I wanted to try it. This was literally the anthem that night playing in the club by Katy Perry, so I'm like why the heck not. My best friend said, "Bert, No!" This lifestyle isn't for you. I've never felt so disappointed and rejected in my life.

I'm sharing this moment because **no one** wanted me. I just wanted to feel love and fill a void that was clear and evident in my heart. I wanted to feel something. Instead, I felt rejected. I couldn't kiss a girl, I didn't want a boy because of my silence of being raped, and I remember that night wanting to die. I was fading away.

## Attracting the Same Spirits

Here's the thing, I couldn't understand why I attracted the same type of people. I would start over and yet the same thing I'd leave would follow me. I found myself attracting the same type of men. The kind who liked me, called me "Bad" but wanted me for my body. I attracted the kinds that challenged my perversion. The ones that want me to make their fantasy come true. I compared myself to porn stars (though I never watched porn) the guys I chose had an addiction to it. I realized that my father and brother also had an addiction to it, which was why I never watched it.

I'd like to insert here that I attracted the same spirits that lived in me. The same spirits that were sown as a seed at age 5. The same spirits that got stronger with every day I'd keep my mouth shut. The same spirits that taught me how to please its lust. The same spirit in the girls who were molested or raped in their childhood were in me. I began to meet the same spirits but through different people. My brokenness attracted broken and vulnerable people. Broken people who want love but can't reach it because of their reality that wasn't the Truth. This is perversion.

Perversion is that ugly, lying, no good spirit that doesn't have a respect for persons, gender, age, orientation, none of that. Perversion is that darkness that masks itself in pride, fear, and every other toxic and damaging emotions. How? Because perversion is the darkness that causes you to be blind to the truth. There is reality (the world that is shaped by your experiences and environments) and then there is Truth (the way things are intended to be).

There is the Spirit of Truth which is Our Father, but there is also the standard of truth. What does God say about you? Every lie that was ever told, God has already spoken the answer/standard of truth over your life. So, when I was listening to perversion, I believed I was ugly, I was fat, I was no good, I was stink, no one would ever love me, but the Lord said I was beautiful, I am peculiar, I am wonderfully made. I didn't know that back then. I'm learning this now. Prior to making it to this moment of learning the difference between reality and truth, I was still imprisoned.

## Dancing with Suicide

I was living in a dark and cold world. I found myself contemplating whether I would jump off the ship. I danced with suicidal thoughts while wondering if anyone would miss me. I found that a smile could hide me, but my soul was rotting. I found that I was stinky, filthy, I was broken and dangerous.

I had to realize that running away from home was the beginning of a process that would take me to my breaking point repeatedly. I found that I had to fight through what people would call mental illnesses but I call it the taunting of spirits. I was depressed, I was filled with fear, I was being squeezed by a python, the enemy was really after me. I was raped, I was molested, I was broken, things I couldn't confess at the time. Things that pride wouldn't allow me to breakthrough.

I did feel abandoned and rejected. I did feel cheap and inexpensive, all lies that internalized. I didn't think I deserved real love and true happiness. I thought those were just fairytales. I even planned a wedding I'll never have. Who could handle me? Who would want me? Who could love me? Who could see beyond my smile? Who could see beyond a fat booty and small waist? Who could see ME for ME? Who could handle my skeletons? Who would stick around if I told them what baggage I came with?

I stayed to myself. I didn't want a man, I didn't want a boyfriend. I didn't want a title. I just wanted to scratch that itch of pleasure from time to time. I did lose my virginity once I was in the military. I did it because I thought it would fulfill me. I thought I was grown enough now, let's see what the big deal was. I found out that I wasn't missing anything. The only difference was I chose who I did it with..

I did start drinking underage. I stopped when I almost got raped by a woman and her fiancé. I was drunk and I heard them plotting that I was going to get "F'd tonight!" I woke up from drunkenville and drove home in second to third gear (I drove at five speeds, that I learned how to drive in with my dad back then), until I made it home safe.

I did get raped by a married man that I dance around with, who taught me things that I should have only learned because of my husband. I did dance around with the thoughts of being with the same sex. I mean what's the worst that could have happened. I had already gone through everything, right?

I just wanted to be loved. All I wanted was someone to hold me close and not drop me. I've been dropped way too many times, but Who WOULD

WANT ME? WHO WOULD SEE ME. Not who I presented but me, the little girl that was in the cage? Who would help me come out to find my true identity?

I didn't think it was possible? I didn't think that there was a man for me. I tried to date. I tried to love. I tried to have sex because I desired intimacy. However, every touch would send a grenade off in my body. I would freeze because I could only see traumas. This caused me to hate sex. I was afraid of it but my body desired it. Those feelings I felt at age five were getting stronger and stronger. I screamed for attention, but my body was the only thing that I knew that could give me the attention that I thought I wanted. The attention that I knew would gain a response that I see, if you catch my drift. I could see an arousal, but I couldn't feel a thing.

I desired for someone to get to know me.

Not for my body, but I felt that's all that I have to gain the attention of dudes. I desired intimacy and oneness. Who would get intimate with me? Who would want to know my thoughts? Who would learn about my intelligence? Who would know that I'm really lame and enjoy science and chemistry? That I'm really not ratchet nor hood, just a girl who wanted to experience her youth because my childhood and innocence was robbed.

I didn't have a real community. I knew how to get by but I never really fit in. I was a great performer. I kept a great act going on and I believed it. Truth is, I was in a narrative that was never intended for my life. Traumas and dark places wrote my script. Even when I tried to see the light, the light was manipulated.

It was rooted in a response that kept those dark spirits employed. I'll dive more into this later.

How can I find love when I'm broken? What is love? What is life? Who would want to spend the rest of their life with me? ME! Not the person I can be but me? Truth is, I didn't know who I was anymore and I didn't think anyone would miss me if I "slipped" off the back of the fantail (the back of the ship)

## I'm Glad I didn't Jump

I contemplated suicide a lot on deployment. I was losing my marbles. My demeanor at work changed. I stopped caring about my weight, hair, the excellence in my job, I was over it all. One night on the ship, I went down to one of my spaces that I turned into a studio and cried out to God loudly. This was the day I opened my Bible and made a vow with God. I told the Lord that if he doesn't show up in my life right now, I will end my life. I cried out, I worshipped from my core. I had one song on repeat, "The Blessings of Abraham," by Donald Lawrence the slow version. The song was reminding me that the Lord has it all under control. Then, I began speaking in tongues and it was different. It was powerful, I heard the Lord. Not in the sound of Mufasa, but I heard the voice of God.

The Lord began to share with me the purpose of my life, the reason why I'm fighting and I asked the Lord to be a prophet. I didn't know what that meant, but from my understanding, a prophet spoke to God and had a relationship so that's what I coveted. I also asked the Lord to reveal to me my husband. I told him if he shows me who he is, I'll surrender everything. My best friend was actually recording in the studio the encounter to witness this moment.

That night I had a dream about my friend Sam. That's when I knew I needed to wait for him. That moment I had such a powerful encounter with the Lord, made me want to get to know God even more. I had hope that the Lord was real and now, you couldn't tell me otherwise. I just wanted to be attached to something that was greater than myself. Being a science nerd, I knew there had to be greater. I want to get to know the Creator of creation. I grew up churched, so I expected God to come in a churchy way, but I found out that night that there was more to God than what I imagined.

# Chapter 9

*"The Start of a Process"*

Between 19 and 22, I was in a serious process. I had to learn how to live without my parents. I had to adopt a new lifestyle according to Navy standards. I would meet sailors from all across the globe who helped me grow beyond my small-town mentality. I would make life-long friends from different walks of life. I would leave the city of Chicago, to move to the city of Norfolk. I would find myself homesick and I would travel back every weekend to get my dysfunctional fix.

I made friends in Norfolk but my heart was where comfort was. I wanted to run away from home but I couldn't stay away. Truth is, my trauma became normal and I was willing to break the rules to be "normal." I'd travel outside the 300mi radius to please everyone. I battled the comments from my family members that told me I was changing. I wanted to satisfy my mom because her desires were for me to come home every free weekend I could. I wanted to make my mom happy and she had a powerful voice and influence that maneuvered my life. I couldn't define the powerful influence she had over me as control until I began to embrace that I was changing. I would travel for long hours to a place that I so desperately wanted to get away from.

My friends were beginning to complain that I was going home too much. They told me that I have to grow up. They had no idea how conflicting that statement was for me. I was being pulled in a game of tug of war. In one direction, South Carolina was my stronghold. I wanted my hometown to be proud of me, and see me as someone to look up to. On the other arm, I was beginning to be introduced to the future. The future of Tre'elle. When I came home, I began to feel like I was missing out on many opportunities to become my own woman. Truth be told, the war was with my past and my future. When I was in Beaufort, I was still the twelve-year-old girl that obeyed my parents, even though I'm grown living three states away. When I was in Norfolk, I was a young woman who explored the city that had way more to offer. I had to take control of my life.

## Taking Control

At the age of 19, I began to develop an independent woman attitude. I decided at the age of 19 to rebel against the things I was taught that were "wrong." I'd get my first tattoo on my birthday. It was a Hello Kitty head on my thigh. That was the age where I lost my virginity "officially," to a friend who had no interest in my body, but I gave it to him. Something clicked in me where I wanted to do something that I wanted to do. I didn't know how dangerous that gesture was. I was finally taking control of my life.

This control thing ran deep. That night I lost my virginity, I awoke many spirits that have been lying dormant. The spirit of manipulation, control to avoid being rejected and alone. I learned how to use my body to get what I want and this was not limited to sex but quality time. This behavior developed as my way to control situations that I couldn't control in the past. I blindly began treating people like how I was treated. I also discovered after losing my virginity, that sex would break me down. I never enjoyed it. Gestures would send me in a downhill spiral. I would find that if I gave my body to someone, they would be engaging with my traumas. They would go inside me only to feel my pain, my hurt, and my fight for my life because my mind was no longer there. They would feel my body's response to what I was doing previously in my life.

I appeared to be very experienced during sex because I did have experience in certain departments.

*Side note. Have you wondered how people learned what they know? When engaging in sexual behaviors at such a young age, like how did you learn this? Who taught you this? Was in through porn or did this happen to you? How many experiences are you bringing into this experience?*

At that age, I knew how to do things that the guys in my age group never experienced. It would make them fall in love (really lust). I was using my body as a way to spread this perverted behavior to other men. I felt like I could take their souls with sex. I was very mature and possessed a power that was scary. I'll discuss the dangers of me later in this text. However, I found that in my independent mindset to take control of my life, I would also learn how to control others.

## Control Controlled Me

The control that once controlled me, had now manifested in me to control others. I was a vessel to be used because I was broken. I didn't know that I was making dudes fall in love with me through my actions. My actions weren't always revealed in sex. It was through time and attention. Truth moment, I didn't sleep with a lot of guys, my numbers were very low because sexual pleasure would come at the cost of my sanity. Traumas would spring up with every trigger through touch. I didn't like what I was doing. I didn't like what I felt on the inside of me. Me exercising abstinence (most the time) was a way to control my dangerous self. It kept the beast in me tamed for the most part. It was the first time I believe I exercised self-control. I had to go cold turkey. I would tell guys to stay away from me, trust me this is for your own good. Though they didn't understand it.

I made guys care about me or fall in lust with me because I was being "me." However, I struggled with my identity. What does being me mean? Truthfully, the control in me knew what to say to keep them close to give me attention that I desired so that I won't feel alone in abandoned as I felt in my childhood. The control in me could pull from my archives in my filing cabinet and be the girl I knew you wanted me to be. I was a chameleon. I was the girl that could be in the room who used my experience to fit in but never fit in. For example, I played basketball in high school from 10th to 12th grade. I spent three years of learning how to turn my overweight body into an athlete. So, I could hoop with the fellas and I was pretty good. So, when I'm around guys, I could talk about sports, and I could take you out on the court and ball for real.

This was my story for the next 10 years. I had to unlearn and I'm still unlearning unhealthy habits that became my norm. How to get what I want was something that I mastered. For men, I don't want you, I only wanted what you can give me, which was time and attention. Time and attention was the "sex" I desired. I wanted to feel loved or desired. In exchange, I would give you good vibes and dope energy. I'll be your home girl, I could be whatever role you'd like. I learned how to listen and if I'm in your life, I will get what I want by being available and that listening ear. I would rock with you, I'll be your ride or die. I'll be loyal to you and I'll be your best friend. What else? I can be what you want me to be because that is what I was groomed to be since childhood.

*Typing this now is bringing me through deliverance.*

You see, I learned how to mask and hide really well through my smile.

*Fun Fact, I didn't like my smile. I had a fake tooth because I chipped it skating at the skating rink when I was 6-years-old. For 10 years I dealt with a temporary tooth that would get a stain on it. I would get cracked on (teased)  until I got my*

*permanent one that was also too big and it didn't match.*

Yet, people loved it so. Anyways,  I could be what you wanted me to project. Yet, I was drowning in my identity that was still locked in the cave.

Once again, I controlled people with great intentions but it left me broken every time. When people would leave me, I would shatter. I'd suffer from every emotional wound that I haven't dealt with nor did I heal from. I over extended myself in relationships and I would begin to measure all that I've done for the individual who'd leave and I'd go crazy. I would soon learn that my giving was my way to control. I would find that I could only be as good in a relationship if I gave. If I said, no, the relationship was gone. It was built on what I could do and how I could serve. My serving was perverted. Relationships would start out really well and then if I detect a change and I'd try to overcompensate to make sure I'm secured. This type of behavior left me shallow. I didn't have the capacity to go deep because I was drained spiritually, emotionally, sometimes financially, because I would give.

This was a learned behavior that I had to unlearn. I had to begin to ask myself at the age of 30, why am I giving up my time, energy, and resources so easily? I would pour all that I am in exchange for my broken love language of time and attention. As I mentioned before, I developed people-pleasing and this was something that I had to be delivered from. This was what my relationships were. The only person who should have that amount of access and control was and is God. I had this fear of disappointment. I never wanted to disappoint anyone who was in my life. So, in my pleasing and "serving" I'd do my best to keep my friends happy and the expense of my peace. My loyalty became a stronghold to dead things that the Lord wanted to rip out of me.

So, let me confess this while I'm in this vain, yes, I learned how to be a 'master' manipulator in the field that I was in. I learned how to make people fall in love with me from me being "me" or who I projected to be. When I didn't have more of "me" to give, I was replaced. My manipulation applied to anyone. No one was safe from my toxicity. I treated men like how I wanted to treat the men in my life who molested me and caused me trauma but innocent guys became a victim to my brokenness and control. I didn't care for women because I've been dropped by so many times. I was dropped because of my disappointments and unrealistic expectations that I placed women who meant a great deal to me.

I treated women like how I wanted to be treated because of the things I lacked. I used nurturing relationships as a temporary bandage to heal my bottomless pits of brokenness. If you were a nurturer or someone who gave me attention, I'm yours and available to be taken advantage of. Use me, rape me, take all that I have, but as you take advantage of me, I'm getting what I want, which is attention and time.

**I was still selling myself for rockets,**

which were now temporary moments of pleasure that never lasted long. My traumas took root. The rockets I gave as a child manifested into my need for time and attention. I was no longer taunted by a single spirit. I now had a community of spirits within me. My traumas, silence, and fear caused the perfect breeding grounds to invite other spirits in. They were having a party in me while I'm dying and being tormented in my thoughts and sleep. I was a walking cesspool of demonic forces that controlled me.

I was an independent woman. I felt like I didn't need anyone to make me successful. I could control that success that I had in the military by controlling my behavior. Yes, I had early promotable evaluations, which helped me get advanced quickly. I could control my career and its outcome. All I had to do was study, work hard, stay in shape, pass an exam, and I'm the world's best sailor. This was a learned behavior as well. This was something I developed through trauma. Remember earlier, I mentioned that I was a smart girl. My trauma taught me how to stay in books, stay out the way, and set goals to be the best to take my mind off of my mess.

This was proof that my trauma and demonic oppression manifested. They were no longer seeds, not even a house but a castle. What once were tormenting thoughts became oppressing actions. The real me was snatched in a cave somewhere waiting for a hero or for someone to rescue her, while the fake me, the projection of me, the projection of how I wanted to be seen, the mirage of me that I allowed people to see was all a bunch of sugar honey ice tea. I would get mad that no one could see me. I would be angry with myself when I genuinely wanted something but my toxic self won't allow me to enjoy anything.

My perverted lens robbed me of the goodness of things that were really good for me but I couldn't see it. Truth is I was afraid of people now, but most importantly afraid of myself of what I could do. I had a power that was evil in me. That controlling power to get what I want. Using my pain to fuel me to move in unclean ways. I was controlled psychologically, sexually, emotionally, all of me was controlled in my childhood. I hated it, but couldn't see at the time, the projection of those things in my young adult life.

# Chapter 10

*"Control is a Bleep"*

Control is a monster but it isn't always negative. Some things are inline to protect you. Yet, when control is negative we find it's rooted in witchcraft. Many scriptures in the Bible tell us so. In a bible plan I read, it gave some examples of the manifestations of control, one example mentioned that one way to know that you suffer from control is when anxiety shows up when things are not going your way, or when someone doesn't do what we ask. Yes me, I'm guilty.

Maybe things aren't perfect in our lives, so we develop OCD like behaviors. Truth is OCD is rooted in control. Things could be slipping in your life and the only thing you can control is sorting the colors of

M&Ms, or keeping a clean house when nothing is out of order. Fixing up broken things to feel like you've restored something and had the power to make something that was once rugged beautiful according to your standard. Hm.

I also found that over-explaining could be a root. I was on both ends of things. But how was I able to let go of control was first to Confess I had a control issue as well. I prayed to God to be rid of the controls' grip over my life. I couldn't take it anymore. This prayer came because I was honestly tired of my mom's grip over me. As I prayed to be loosened from her grip, the Lord showed me, me. Not her, **ME**. I had to come to terms with the fact that I hated no. I only wanted yes's. If I got a no, I would manipulate my way to a yes. I'll keep asking, I'll be persistent and that was control.

I over-explained and it's because I didn't want others to have a bad image of me. No matter what my words were, they were never enough. The individual still thought what they wanted to think but me over explaining was a way to control what others thought of me. I wanted people to see me the way I portrayed myself. I wanted things to go like how I planned in my head. I would have a movie running in my brain of how the days should go and when it didn't turn out right I would catch a fit, like a real big tantrum.

My inability to control affected my mood. My emotions would run rapidly. I didn't know how to be. I was always anxious. Though the Bible tells us not to be anxious in anything. Truth is, I wanted to control men, women, and my surroundings. I wanted boys to like me but not fall in love with me because I didn't want to take it a step further. I learned how to listen, so I could find things that I could control.

Yet, I'm just being me, but there was a switch that was in me that would be on auto so that it would trip if things weren't going according to my perfect plan. If I couldn't have you, well, that wasn't an option. I could make you want me. All I had to do was reveal from my archive of experiences to have you in my hand. Once again, my traumas made me toxic even when I tried to come from a good place. I had become an **unstable isotope.**

# Chapter 11

*"The Unstable Isotope"*

Allow me to define perversion real quick. The definition of perversion according to Google is "the alteration of something from its original course, meaning, or state to a distortion or corruption of what was first intended." I can sum that up in six words, "The opposite of what God intended." God has a unique design and intention for everything. When he made creation, He saw that everything he made was and is good. The only thing that wasn't good was for man to be alone. Otherwise, everything was pure and authentic.

When perversion crept in and was acted upon, the pure lifeline was altered by another path. This path was the path that God warned his two greatest creations about. Do not eat of the fruit of knowledge of good and evil. It was never meant for us to become knowledgeable of the enemy's tactics. Yet, we are here. When something goes the opposite of what God desires or ordained to be good, it's not good and it is perverted. Perversion is a lie and opposite of what the Lord said.

I was arrested by perversion and I was trapped in a perverse prison. I was unable to see myself in the way God did. I thought I was ugly, unattractive, fat. I didn't believe I deserved happiness and great things out of life. I didn't believe in myself, though people saw glimpses of great things in me. I could achieve anything I set my mind to do except for the things that were meant for me. I could help others come out of a cave while I was still sinking in quick-sand. I could see the positive things in others but be blinded to the precious stones in me. I could do the works of the Lord but still, be bound in chains. I was anointed but the Spirit of God didn't dwell in me always, more like a pass through type of thing because I had a lot of work to be done. I was the true definition of His gift coming without repentance.

I was drowning in my sin, in my secrets, and in my relationships. I wasn't happy, though I appeared to be. My emotions were unstable. My traumas were winning. My soul was rotting and no one could see it. I was an unstable isotope. My life was spiraling out of control inwardly, yet on the exterior, I had it all.

I had a dope military career. I drove a Lexus at 20 (influenced as well), I had money in the bank, I was responsible, I made my parents proud, I was the model citizen, but I had issues. I was fighting in my sleep. I wasn't getting rest. I was being tormented. I didn't want to sleep by myself. I needed companion-ship. I desired intimacy. I wanted someone to know me for me, or help me discover me. I brought dudes in my bed only to tell them to leave before anything could start. I was flip floppy in my emotions. I'll call people I really didn't want to talk to only to pass time. I'd spend hours on the phone having idle conversations. I also suffered from anxiety attacks back to back.

The many men that were interested in me, I would warn them that they cannot handle me. They always thought that sex was what I was talking about. If they tried to pursue me, I would control the situation. I'd control whether or not you get any attention or some attention depending on how I was feeling at the time. Once again, an unstable isotope.

## What's an Isotope

Allow me to explain to you the science of an isotope and how it applies to this moment. An isotope is composed of the same element and the same atomic number but differs in the mass number due to the neutrons or different nuclear properties. The chemical properties are the same, but the nuclei are different. Depending on the nucleus some isotopes can be harmless and others can become radioactive. Two of the same elements can weigh the same but depending on what is in the nucleus or the core of the element determines its stability. When there is too much in the nucleus, the element becomes unstable, it begins to corrode and emit radiation, which is toxic.

A great example would be Carbon-12 and Carbon-14. Carbon-12 is considered a stable isotope because it has the same amount of protons and neutrons which is 6. This gives Carbon-12 the mass of twelve, which is balanced. However, Carbon-14 is considered radioactive (unstable) because there's 6 protons and 8 neutrons in the atom causing the mass (or the weight) of the carbon atom to be 14 and be radioactive. I wanted to be carbon 12. I wanted to be stable but there was a castle of spirits in me, my nucleus was heavy and my burden caused me to be radioactive.

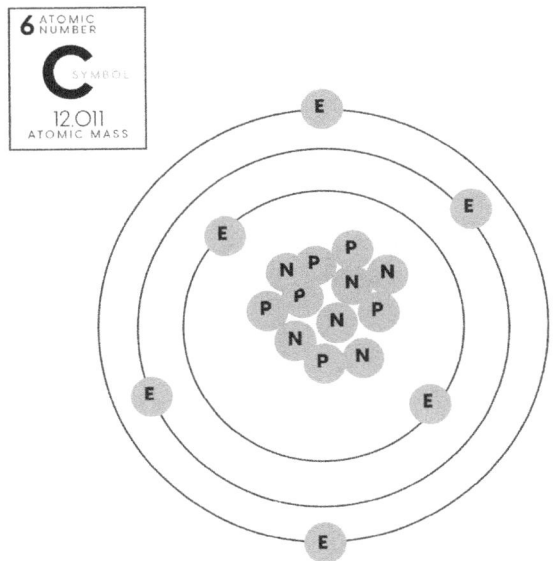

**P = PROTONS | E = ELECTRONS | N = NEUTRONS**

*Example of Carbon 12: There's 6 protons and 6 neutrons in the atom. This is a stable isotope.*

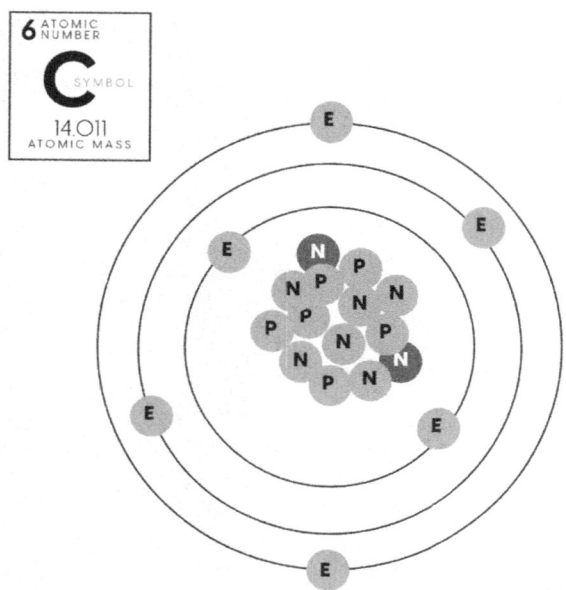

**6** ATOMIC NUMBER

**C** SYMBOL

14.011
ATOMIC MASS

**P=PROTONS | E=ELECTRONS | N=NEUTRONS**

*Example of Carbon 12: There's 6 protons and 8 neutrons in the atom. This is an unstable isotope. The atom has more mass in the atom which causes it to be radioactive.*

The Lord desires for us to be balanced. We were never meant to be unstable in our ways. He asks that we renew our hearts and minds daily. He gives us ways to obtain peace if we just keep our minds stayed on him. He gives us all the elements (protons) we need to stay whole. Yet, the evil one would come to add more weight to your nucleus. He desires to sift you and make his way to your heart by giving you a weight that you cannot carry on your own. He causes your heart (nucleus) to become burdened with traumas and pain. Your atomic number which is our purpose and identity cannot handle that mass. Therefore, you will become unstable in all of your ways.

Yes, I was filled with radiation. I emitted that bad energy on others, who didn't know. I was used once again to break people, just like that moment in the bathtub with my cousin. I was able to move like the rest of the stable atoms moved, but I had a dark side. I had a side in me that was filled with holes. This was my brokenness. That brokenness became pockets to store heavy weights and burdens in my heart. My chambers were blocked and I was dangerous.

## The Dangers of Me

I couldn't be trusted with my emotions. I didn't trust myself. I was unstable in my ways, unable to make tough choices. I had a reprobate mind. I danced around with possibilities and alternate realities because my past allowed me to create fantasies because of things that I endured to ease my crazy. I could foresee my desires and play out every possible outcome and be prepared for every last one. I was engaged in the battle/war of my mind. I fought tirelessly for my sanity. I fought to choose God every time and yet I failed on many occasions. I'd be consumed by a weight that I couldn't bear.

As I confess these things now, I am becoming more aware of the times in my life where I was used. As I stated above, I learned how to be controlled and how to control. I learned how to manipulate. I learned how to play the roles so well, that I could be a great performer and was completely unaware of how I slipped into dark moments.

I could be loyal to you. I'll be your ride or die. I'll be your best friend. I'll keep all your secrets. I'll listen to you well. Well enough, so I can learn how to play my hands. I could buy you what you want, I could give you the attention. I wasn't asking for much in return, I just found the pleasure in control.

I confess these things again because I didn't know that this was how my traumas were manifesting. I was always seen as strong, but I was also weak. I learned how to play the number two in moments where someone was stronger than me. I could be submissive and lead from the passenger side. As long as I had someone near, I was fine. As long as I'm not alone, as long as there is time and attention for me then I'm okay. As long as my desire for intimacy met.

# Chapter 12

There are actually four types of intimacy, emotional, intellectual, sexual, and experimental. Sharing ideas and thoughts are intellectual conversations that can be reached through the mind. Emotional is the vulnerability piece that causes you to share your emotions and feelings. Experimental is the bonding that takes place through activities like going to concerts, fishing, etc. Then, there's sexual intimacy, which is a deeper expression of emotions and connectedness with another person.

In my pursuit to feel complete, I needed all four types of intimacies. I had an array of people who were around me that could give me each type of intimacy. I depended on my friends for the intellectual, experimental, and emotional parts of me. I enjoyed going out, turning up, having fun, and doing things that tick-led my fancy. I was an all around types of people who can find a good time in anything. Whether this is a 5k, a concert, playing basketball, going out to a club, per-forming in a club (poetry and music), going to music festivals, I had those groups of people who I could do those things with.

Intellectually, I needed a challenge. I love sci-ence and technology. I was a nerd in school. I read books all the time. I went to college, I have two degrees, many certifications, but I continue to pursue knowledge and understanding of life around me. I love deep talks because I'm a deep person. A real thinker and ques-tioner. I questioned why all the time. My intellectual curiosity had to be challenged by people who were ex-perts in whatever field I was interested in. I challenged myself to learn and I never took the easy route because I found satisfaction in defeating my fears of the unknown.

Emotionally, I had friends where I could vent. We'd shared similar pains, traumas, experiences, and stories. I found those types of relationships were the danger zone for me. If we shared similar things, a bond would be created, a soul tie, a connection that ran deep, and this is where I became a black hole. If I connected to you due to emotions, I fell hard in love. This is where I cracked. This is where I bleed. This is where everything that I keep hidden from others would show up. I'd engage in pouring out all of who I am because I understand. I turned into a super friend. The one to be there for you, but this is also where I'd break because I get taken advantage of. This is the relationship where I would open up to be raped.

These were the types of bonds that would cause me to want to be the savior or superhero. I desperately wanted people to experience freedom even if that means I'm still in the cage. I wanted to push people to a place that I haven't experienced before. I would emotionally be so invested in the lives of others and gain the satisfaction of them achieving and learning and growing hoping that when they get there, they'll remember to grab my hands to bring me out. When that didn't happen, I'd be angry, I'd be in rage. I'd then try to control the situation. I'd be that motivator and encourager, that light. But it was never enough. That would be the point where I would fall and crack just to bleed all over again.

These types of relationships revealed that I needed to be whole. It revealed that I needed healing. It proved that I needed some work. I wanted one person to fill a void that couldn't be filled. I put my heart in the hands of people who were still broken. I had to go to the root of these behaviors. I needed to see that it wasn't everyone else fault. It was me. I had to come out of the place of playing victim in order to find victory. Intimacy for me was destroyed since childhood, but I had hope that it could be restored. I had to get to the place where I won't allow these unhealthy patterns to continue in my life. Not anymore, no not this time.

## Not This Time

As my husband and I discussed this segment of the book, he asked me if I controlled him to make him fall in love with me. He did meet me at the most dangerous point of my life. However, I could stand firm and tell him, No. It's because he saw through all my sugar honey ice tea! He showed me something new. I didn't have to try with him. I could be myself around him, whatever that was. I didn't have to put on a front. I revealed my childlike behaviors that he enjoyed. I tried to test the waters to see if he was sexually attracted to me but he denied me.

Truth is, he left me perplexed. I thought he was dysfunctional. I tried to entice him but none of my perverted gestures worked. I was confused. Yet, I was falling in love with him from an emotional place. He was the one I shared all of my feelings with. I was falling for him because he was the one I shared a lot of experimental intimacy with. We'd go to the Guitar centers and plays. We'd sing and play music all the time. I couldn't get him out of head because we shared a lot of intellectual conversations. He was the beginning of breaking me free from this mess. This was the development of our friendship. I'll share more about us later.

Sam showed me something I've never experienced before and that was a healthy relationship. He saw through me, to see me. He witnessed my good heart and soul, but he couldn't see the war that I battled within myself. Many of my friends couldn't see it. I would find myself battling with my thoughts, my ways, my incompleteness and my identity. I struggled and fumbled and I was at my breaking point.

# Chapter 13

*"My breaking point"*

In 2011, I was on one of the longest deployments in history. 10.5 months out to sea. I left in March 2011, we returned in February 2012. While I was out to sea, I entertained a spirit that was stronger than me that I couldn't control. I was like a child playing with fire and I wanted to see how close I could get before getting burned. The spirit would manifest in one of my friends. He was a married man, who told me that he and his wife had an agreement while he was away on deployment. The agreement was he and his wife could do whatever they wanted to do, as long as no one popped up pregnant nor contracted an STD. I brushed this statement off because we were never going to cross that line. I had morals and boundaries. So, I thought.

What attracted me to this guy from the outside looking in was his love for music. He was a musician and he could sing, so we had some things in common. I was immediately attracted to his giftings. I felt he was Sam's replacement and I'm like praise God, I have another homie who understands me. He was tall, not the best looking apple in the bunch but he had a stunning personality. He was corny (not popular, not into fashion or anything) and very intelligent. He was an IT (Information Technology) on the ship, therefore we were in the same department. We could speak techy talk. He'd be the bridge to help me learn more as an IC (Interior Communications). We spent a lot of time together. When we weren't working, we'd be in the chapel singing or in one of my shops recording music. Those were the things I saw initially in my friend.

What I didn't see at the time was what rested beneath all initial attractions that caused us to be great friends. I had gotten comfortable. I allowed myself to let my hair down. I was getting the time and attention, great conversations that hit the marks of my love languages. We'd share many of the intimacies from experimental, emotional, and intellectual. I didn't see deeper than that. I didn't see that it was a trap. I wanted to believe in him. I wanted to believe that he'd never hurt me. I wanted to believe that I was safe but I wasn't. The moment I let my guard down, were the moments my past and every other spirit awakened.

This dude was Satan without horns and used at that time. This is a big claim to make but it was my truth. Once again, he could sing, play many instruments, and he knew the Word as well. Yet, he had many cracks. He was just as unstable as I was. He was the sly fox. He knew what to say and when to say it. He knew how to listen, he knew how to control. The same things I could do, he could do better. He knew how to make me laugh, he was loyal, but it came at a cost.

I opened myself to a friend, who I said I would never cross the lines for. You'd think he was my boat boo but he wasn't. We enjoyed one another's company. I met his wife and daughter (prior to deployment) and they were so sweet. I felt this was all good, but it was a trap. I was being entangled and didn't know it. He got me right where he wanted me. I was open and available because I was receiving what I wanted time and attention.

As I mentioned before, I would give you all of me if you gave me what I wanted which was time and attention. I didn't ask for things. I knew gifts came at a cost. If I received anything, it was in rockets, or something that could be used to control me and my happiness. So, yes, I was getting what I wanted.

The first time he tried me, I knew he was interested. He fell in the category with every other man, except my husband, then friend, Sam. I brushed it off, I told him no, it's not like that. However, in the back of my mind, it woke up control and my need for sexual intimacy. I had ignored sex for quite sometime so, it woke up that feeling again. I brushed it off and hoped that it wouldn't continue but I was curious. Our conversations also shifted from music and general stuff, to sex. I was now engaging in sexual intimacy through the exchange of words.

The guy from the ship started asking me questions about sexual gestures and asked if I've done them before. Now, I've done some crazy things but nothing like what he implied. He'd explain what it was like and how to do it. Those questions became seeds of curiosity. Those seeds made me wonder if it was true. I began to dance with the pleasurable feelings that would make me have the feelings of arousal. I would mask these feelings by writing erotic poetry. I didn't have the courage to do it in real life. So, writing was a release. Until, it was no longer sufficient.

My curiosity bursted, and the door was opened. He was waiting. I started allowing him to do things to me, slowly but surely. He took his time with me. We started with kisses and touches. I'd run away and say no, but I'd be lying to myself because I knew in my body I wanted *it*. I had feelings for him and it wasn't love. It was lust. I was initially attracted to his gifts, but our spirits knew one another. We both battled with lust, which opened the door to fornication and adultery. My standard went from no you can't touch me, to you can but not here. Those questions he asked me would be answered and he was the answer. I wouldn't allow him to go all in, but we'd foreplay like crazy. Does this sound familiar to you?

I attracted my past. I complied like a little child. I was in the sunken place and I didn't know how to get out of it. Even though I was on a journey to God, I still wasn't anchored because I wasn't healed. I was in an ocean being tossed to and fro because I wanted to control my healing. So, I allowed God some room, but my grip was still on it and you see where that led me. I changed my standards often. I wasn't innocent, even if I portrayed myself to be. I didn't want to go all the way with him. I did everything but everything else. This guy was the manifestation of the spirits I've encountered in my past. I did the exact same thing. I became a little 10-year-old girl to this guy who was older than me. I was back at "home" making up excuses, saying I'll never let it happen again but it did.

———————

Our ship pulled into Palma, Spain. I was officially 21-years old. Palma was great! This place was Cancun, Mexico during spring break during the summer. Nude beaches and alcohol everywhere. I was legal to drink and I wanted to celebrate. One of those days in port, my liberty buddy was that guy. He was kind and nice. He bought me and my homegirl drinks all day. Our last shot was four horsemen, but the bartender made it more like ten. It was like 6 or 7 different brands of dark liquor, mixed together and poured in a double shot glass. That was the shot that tipped me over. He told me he had a hotel room where I could change clothes on the beach. I agreed but didn't really feel good about it. I didn't feel good about anything at this point. I was drunk drunk! I was able to walk but I was done, beyond lit.

While my homegirl was in the bathroom changing, my friend came on top of me. I froze and it wasn't because I was drunk, I froze because I knew what was about to happen. This guy took my wrap off and moved my bottom from my two piece bathing suit.

He began to enjoy a meal that was burning me on the inside. When he was full he'd then go all the way. I was getting deep stroked by this guy who I could no longer stand. I was laying on the bed in tears but I didn't put up a fight. He was looking in my face talking sugar honey iced tea. He said things that I couldn't respond to. No, I didn't want him, but I was barely fighting in my actions to tell him to get off of me. I was just laying there taking it. I was battling more so in my mind. If that wasn't enough, my homegirl came out of the bathroom and he tried to get her to join. She declines and walks to the balcony without understanding my torment. She thought I wanted it, she knew our little history so, I don't blame her.

This was my worst nightmare. I prayed to God to let this be over or give me strength because I was too drunk to fight. I kicked him off of me, I grabbed my homegirl who was out of it and ran to the beach where the rest of the crew was. I drank and tried to drown myself in alcohol but couldn't get drunk. My best friend saw me and knew something was wrong. She took me back to the ship and I had to stay there and wallow in my pain. I never said anything.

I didn't tell my chain of command, but they noticed a change in my behavior. I had given up on myself. I couldn't do it anymore. I couldn't protect myself so who will? God, where are you now? I wanted to jump off of the ship for real. I don't have anyone, I'm in a mental prison and it got worse. My past caught up to my present and I could no longer see a future. I lost hope. I shut down. I was depressed. It was July, we didn't come home until February. I had a tough road ahead of me. I couldn't run anymore. I reached my breaking point and I finally snapped. I snapped back to the place I needed to be in. I needed God like never before. I left a piece of me in Palma de Mallorca. Out with the old and in with the new.

### I ran into Healing

Our ship pulled out of Palma and we were back out to sea. I disappeared in broad daylight on the ship. No one saw me, not even the guy who did this to me. I had to switch my routines. I stayed below decks. I worked even harder than ever. I rose above the pain and channeled the superstar me. I screamed and cried but this was the beginning of my healing. I had officially reached my lowest point in life. There was no way I could come out of this on my own.

This was the best moment of my life. This was the moment where God rose in me. This was the beginning of the next 9 years of my life. Things are about to go up from here. I would soon come back to my best friend who became my husband. We would soon have four kids, a beautiful home, and be the next couple goals. I would soon find out that deliverance is necessary. My ugliness was about to be revealed. I would soon see the manifestation of spirits. I would discover my inner afflictions. I would soon endure traumatic birthing experiences with all of my children. I would have to work through my skeletons with some-one who could handle me but didn't know what he was getting himself into. Now is the time for me to become stable again. Now, is the time to fight the toughest fight for my life. My freedom!

# Pt. III

## Deliverance

# *Introduction*

The moment I was touched inappropriately, there was a new path made in my spirit. This path became the scenic route of perversion and its friends. If you can think about the human brain, you'll know that it's a giant muscle, composed of many nerves that signal every thought. It's your body's central processing unit (CPU). It's where the mind lives as well. Yes, there is a difference between the brain and the mind. The brain is simply the response of what the mind tells it. This is why it is said that a mind is a supernatural place. Yet, the brain is the bridge that has the ability to take inputs from the natural and supernatural realm.

The brain is so smart to its own fault. Because it's designed to process and store information, it saves everything into its own category. What is seen, what you are around, what you experience, what you learn, and the functions of what does what, as the list goes on. All of this information is stored whether it's in the front of your mind or in your unconscious. When you experience trauma, believe it or not, the memories are not the only thing that is stored. Spiritual wickedness attaches to the memories as well. The feelings of pleasure and pain, the confusion, all of it is stored and becomes intermixed with one another.

Trauma trips the brain because of the mind's ability to send signals to it. What the brain doesn't know, it will still store it to the best of its ability. I will try to make sense of it and house this information somewhere. More than likely, it will be placed in your unconscious. This is the dark place that psychologists are trying to figure out.

Sigmund Freud, one of the founding fathers of psychology, would use hypnosis to infiltrate the unconscious before moving into psychoanalysis. Carl Jung, another founding father of psychology, would devote his study to reveal the functions of the unconscious through our ego. The point I'm making is the unconscious of your mind is where the brain stores repressed thoughts, memories, emotions. This is where demonic oppression dwells. Yes, spiritual activity that lies dormant, waiting for the right time, the right pressure, and the right atmosphere to erupt. Yet, the poisonous activity from our unconscious seeps into your everyday life. However, what is in the dark must come to the light. This is what deliverance is. Taking the deep dark things and exposing them to the truth.

## The Wheat and the Tares

At this moment I'm reminded of the parable about the wheat and the tares. In Matthew 13:24-30 there is a parable about the wheat and the tares. I'd encourage you to read it for yourself.

> *"Another parable He put forth to them, saying: "The kingdom of heaven is like a man who sowed good seed in his field; but while men slept, his enemy came and sowed tares among the wheat and went his way. But when the grain had sprouted and produced a crop, then the tares also appeared. So the servants of the owner came and said to him, 'Sir, did you not sow good seed in your field? How then does it have tares?' He said to them, 'An enemy has done this.' The servants said to him, 'Do you want us then to go and gather them up?' But he said, 'No, lest while you gather up the tares you also uproot the wheat with*

*them. Let both grow together until the harvest, and at*

*the time of harvest I will say to the reapers, "First*

*gather together the tares and bind them in bundles to*

*burn them, but gather the wheat into my barn."*

I needed you all to read this for yourself. The kingdom of heaven is simply a place where deliverance is, the place where the healer is, the place where there is no torment. This is the dwelling place of God. A place of good and fertile ground. A place that we all have within us and have access to. While the man slept, the enemy sowed tares. I don't know about your traumas and what you went through but there were moments where the enemy came to sow tares in your life.

You've read mine already, so you are now familiar that the enemy was on an assignment to kill me and you since we came on this earth. His assignment is to steal, kill, and destroy. The tares were sown while I was asleep, while I was young and tender. Those seeds of perversion and its friends were stored in my unconscious but began to manifest when God's seed began to bear fruit. Here goes the tares. I wanted to do right, but wrong was always in the midst. All I wanted was to be a great friend. All I wanted to do was love others. I wanted to be pure and cleaned but I wasn't healed. No matter the great things I did or how pure I was, I always went back to my cell of brokenness because I ran away from problems only to face them again and again. I'd place unrealistic expectations to feed my emptiness. While I slept, seeds were sown. While I loved, fruit sprang forth. However, all fruit weren't good fruit.

What I love about the parable with the wheat and the tare is the servant's ability to recognize the tares, as well as, the fruit. Have you ever seen tares and wheat? Google it, they look exactly the same. It takes one who knows God, one who is in a relationship with the Father to see the difference. The farmer told the servant to let them grow together. The farmer understood wisdom. He knew that he did everything he could do well but something went wrong. This had to be the hand of the evil one. So, let tares and the wheat grow, let it manifest, let it tell on itself. Trust me, the tares will speak.

My tares spoke loudly in my responses and reactions to different situations I've faced. The fruit of thoughts and gestures will become a mouth. The non-verbal communications, the feelings within your gut, will scream at you. Good fruit will come forth, but the bad fruits will try to stop it from springing up. That's when you gather them together and allow the kingdom to show up. That's when deliverance shows up. Deliverance acts as the sifting, the great agitator to cause a separation between the two fruits.

Understand that deliverance is a process, as the wheat has to go through a threshing floor. The threshing floor was used to separate the grains from the chaff. When you really want to be healed or delivered, transformed, etc, a process of agitation will occur and there will be a separation required. It's work, but that's when you'll know that the harvest is ready and the time is now. However, You'll have to be one of the few laborers that will work.Those who labor will have the authority, access, and dominion to gather the tares **first**, bind them up in bundles, and burn them.

There will come a time where the enemy will be exposed. There are times where you will speak to the spirits that are bold enough to manifest. It's not until you are delivered and walk in wholeness where you become aware of who and what you are speaking to. Sometimes, that will require you to have to take a step back from everything and really let the Lord search your heart to reveal to you things about yourself that you've never known. Then, you'll be enlightened to know what's really going on.

Let me make this all make sense. The mind is supernatural and powerful. Whatever a man thinks, so is he. Thinking is above the brain. The brain can not conjure a thought, it's a response of its input. The mind is where the magic happens. This is why the enemy attacks it so much. This is why there are so many scriptures that warn you about guarding your mind with the helmet of salvation. This is why the enemy comes so hard because he wants the mind to stay imprisoned. Great wheat is stored in the mind, but so is the tares that are sown through life experience. The mind is the field, and we are to guard it with all of who we are. The tares were strong in me, but I had to continue to endure the process and to be honest, it was only the beginning.

## Inside Out

Remember the movie "Inside out" when Riley took the train of thought to get back to her mind where her emotions dwelled? I'm sorry, I have four kids so, yes, I watch a lot of animated movies. In a scene, Riley's core memory of happiness was gone and now her other emotions try to run Riley like normal. This caused many adverse behaviors in Riley's that her parents, friends, and surroundings recognized.

When traumas began in my life, my brain was just like Riley's emotions. The only difference was I didn't' get rid of Joy. I began to fuel anger, sadness, and fear. Joy was there but she wasn't in charge all of the time. I was this unstable isotope, my brain stored everything, causing me to be thrown off by triggers which were memories that still had feelings and emotions attached to them. My mind was in a war with my emotions and spiritual activity.

My traumas imprisoned me. I only knew the cell that I was in. I had the physical freedom to live my life, but the traumas controlled my CPU. Joy would be in control, but fear would take the wheel. When joy takes control again, Sadness will come in and turn everything blue. Except these weren't limited to emotions I was dealing with. These were spiritual forces that lived in my temple. After the nucleus of my heart became compromised, my mind was the next thing to take over.

The real me was in prison. My correction officers were the emps that would torment me and my warden was Satan's devices. However, my judge was on the throne, waiting to serve an eviction notice to give me my freedom. My righteous judge was saving me and I didn't know it. The same judge that died on the cross was waiting for me. I stayed there in my cell for way too long but it was better late than never. I had to get out of this mindset. I had to be free. Free from the tares and free from the sting of past memories. I didn't like who I was becoming because I knew that wasn't the real me. I no longer wanted to be that girl in the cage. I wanted my freedom.

# Chapter 14

*"My Husband"*

I met my husband, Sam on the ship as we were underway to Haiti at the time due to the earthquake back in 2010. I was 19, young, and excited to leave for my first underway experience. We were at a working party where he was across from me but he was sitting next to this fine dark-skinned guy who I kept looking at. I guess he thought I was looking at him because his tall behind came and sat next to me. I spoke because I didn't want to be rude. I saw we had similar last names "Talbert" and Tolbert. That was the conversation starter.

We knew we weren't related but had the same interest in music. He played the keyboard and would invite me to the ship's chapels to play and hear me sing. This was the beginning of our forever. You can read more about our introduction in his book, "Loving a Fragile Woman," however, I wanted to share that I never imagined that this guy would be my husband and I'd be his wife. I genuinely loved this guy and he was different. Something about him wouldn't allow my perverted toxic unstable isotope self to touch him. He was a beacon of light. He made me smile for real for real. He listened to me and taught me how to trust.

You see I was broken to the point where all things broken became my norm. Anything opposite of that was abnormal. Once again, perverse thinking. In my journey to my husband becoming my man, I had to uncover my skeletons and reveal to him my heart. I had to expose my darkness and bring it to the light. Meeting

Sam would be the beginning of me coming out of my mental prison. Marrying him was the force that kept me out of prison.

I married my husband less than a year later after coming off of deployment. I learned while I was stuck at sea that I could no longer run away from my pain but embrace it. To feel it. To acknowledge it so that I can heal. I had to do a lot of soul work. I had to be alone. I officially went into the wilderness without any plans on ever coming out. Sam was there with me in the wilderness. We were both afflicted with our own skeletons, but there was a love there that was pure and real.

Sam loved me from a light I've never seen. He was patient, kind, trustworthy and respectful. We had a relationship for some time that remained constant. He NEVER disrespected me. He never spoke sex or looked like anything of my past. I feared our love. It was new. I never wanted to put a title to our relationship. It was beyond any boyfriend, girlfriend type of thing. He was my friend and that was enough. I wanted to be his wife, but we never talked about it.

When I came from deployment, I was faced with another test. This test was to allow our relationship to flourish without me being in control. I'd return from leave only to be greeted by Sam's presence on a duty day on the ship. He brought me Taco Bell that night because I missed dinner. This was the night I fell in love. This was the night where I could be and that's it. I thanked him for my food, but that was the night I wanted more. I wanted more than any of the intimacies I desired. I wanted him. All of him. This exceeded sexual gestures, it was a want beyond comprehension. I felt like we were meant to be. This was February 21, 2012. This was the day I fell in love with him.

After that night, we'd go on many months chilling. When I tried to do the most for him, he wouldn't allow me. I'd try to be extra, he'd decline. I tried to throw myself at him sexually but he declined. I thought he wasn't interested in me but that was my inability to process the normal things in life. I began to feel rejected by him because he didn't show me love in the perverse way I was used to. I couldn't control him. Nor did he control me. We chilled and we enjoyed each other until September of 2012. When he asked me to marry him. Of course I agreed to be his forever! In December we'd get married and begin life together.

# The Moments That Shaped Us

Prior to marriage, I was healed to a certain point. I was able to smile and function and really live a life where I was free. When we got married, I thought I'd embrace happily ever after but there were moments that occurred in our marriage that shaped us. While we were enjoying our honeymoon, we conceived our first born. 18 weeks into childbirth, my son was diagnosed with congenitive heart disease.

37-weeks later, he was born at the Children's Hospital of Philadelphia. This moment shook our younger selves. We had to have faith the whole way through. The doctors and nurses mentioned that there was always an option to abort my son at 25-weeks. They told me that there were methods we could take to get it done because there is a high possibility that my child will come out abnormal when he's born. Most babies with heart disease suffer from some type of physical ailments but I didn't care if my child was afflicted, I vowed I would love him through it all.

When I got to Philly, the surgeon kept preparing me for death. They wanted me to know that anything could happen and that they would do their best but there is the possibility of death and more talks of abortion. They kept asking if I was okay because my responses were always, I'm well.

My son was born a few days before my induction date. He needed surgery but a different surgeon from India came in. On the third day after delivery, my child didn't get the heart transplant but the simple surgery that removed the coarctation of his aorta. I'm telling you this not to deviate from me telling my story of walking in wholeness, but that was the moment that truly believe in God. It would be the faith needed to withstand that moment of telling my mom a secret I kept from her for 20 years.

———————————

My children were the best ways for the enemy to get to me. My second child would suffer from seizures. The first attack was scary, she was in my arms and I saw her changing to a bluish color. She looked dead. My husband was working nights at this government facility that wouldn't allow him to have a cell phone. I had to ride in an ambulance with my toddler son, and infant daughter by myself. I was there all night until her fever broke and was able to come home. She would suffer until she grew out of it, really until she was healed, through deliverance. We placed her in the hands of the Lord, and we prayed and fasted and yeah, febrile seizures begone.

Lastly, my twins. I had to get an emergency c-section with the twins. I went into labor at 30 weeks. The twins were about 4lbs a piece. My twins were premature. They spent their time in the NICU until they could come home. I had to see them looking like my oldest son connected to so many machines and this was all too familiar. It hurt because this was the time I wasn't mentally stable. I was alone and under a lot of stress. I had no family to turn to and my husband was unavailable because he worked so much.

I was by myself dealing with so much that I was going to break. The delivery of my twins shook me. I didn't know how I was going to make it. Truth is I was to give up. I was in so much pain because I was allergic to morphine. I was itching, I was throwing up, too weak to fight. My blood pressure was low. I felt like trash.

Bringing the kids home would be a different story. We didn't have much. My twins were preemies so they didn't have clothes, their newborn diapers were too big, and they were really small. They looked like little aliens that needed to develop. I was still in school that wouldn't give me a break. I still had to complete my finals and turn in my assignments online.

So, I'm juggling two little toddlers and newborn twins with an absent husband who's working nonstop to provide for us. We are still sinking fast. Financially, we were okay but the money wasn't enough to run a healthy household. My husband was losing his wife mentally, sexually, emotionally, and physically I was no longer available. I checked out. I became a robot. My children were losing their mom. I was able to provide them with just enough.

With the little that I had left in me, I was able to make sure they were fed. I made sure to pump throughout the day to store milk. I had a little energy to play with them, and I became a teacher mommy so that they could learn. While they took naps I was logged in to do school work. I had to cook dinner for my husband who would sometimes come home just to go to bed and not eat. The house was a mess. My mom would be on FaceTime yelling at me because she could see laundry on my floor. The dishes slept in the sink overnight. I would stay up the remainder of the night to finish school work and I couldn't do it anymore. I couldn't take it. I didn't get any rest and my body started to break down. I started going to the ER because I thought I was dying. Only to find I was suffering from anxiety attacks.

## Fighting for my Life

I was working out trying to do something for myself. Something I could control but then my body gave up on me. I had to stop and I went into a deep depression. No one from the outside could see it but my husband and I could. We were distant. We weren't having any forms of intimacy. We didn't go out because we couldn't find a babysitter who could handle our load. We weren't having any emotional or intellectual conversations because he was working so much. Sex was traumatic and I never had the energy to do so.

My world was closing in on me. Everything was piling up on me. I even documented moments of my anger and tears. I punched through walls. I was very snappy and unhappy. I was overflowing from the memory bank of my emotions and trauma where small things made me explode.

The wheat and the tares sprung forth. I displayed the love of God and was able to serve in the church, and appear whole but the tares showed up at night. While I'm fighting in my sleep heaviness of spirits that would only leave if I called on Jesus' name. Nightmares that would haunt me. I would be running and falling and being consumed by dark entities. I was going crazy. I felt I was like a puppet on a string. Robotic in nature, with no real purpose and an unhealthy brain.

I didn't know what to do anymore. My husband had to adjust to all of my actions. There were times we would have sex and I would freeze. I would cry because he did things that were familiar to my past. If my husband expressed any actions that were similar to my past, I would lock my legs, I'd shake. There were moments where I would silently scream. I would disengage. We'd make love and I'll crawl into the fetal position and cry.

There were some instances we'd go weeks without a single touch. I'd reject him. I didn't want his love. I didn't want his arms around me. I wanted to be alone. Some days, I'll respond to meet his needs but not because I wanted to but because I didn't want him to go anywhere else to get it. There were moments where I couldn't have sex anymore. My body was no longer functioning. I had no juice in the box. My faucet was turned off.

My husband had the complex challenge to love me while making love to my traumas. He had to make love to me through my broken pieces. He had to make love to someone who could never be fully satisfied even if the pleasure was amazing.

My brain pulled from those memories to tell me how to perform in bed but the emotional stench of perversion made its way into my bedroom. I was going to lose my husband. Therefore, I would try to pretend to enjoy sex. Once again, I was a great performer, only to collapse after the curtains closed.

This wasn't the case every night, but there were nights, after making love, I'd go to an alternate world. I'd feel like.I had gotten raped by a man who only wanted to love me and care for me. I would pray for him to hurry up or pray to fight the memories that would flash across my mind? I hated sex, not my husband, I loved him so much.  However, we were drifting apart. He didn't know how to satisfy me, but I didn't know how I could be satisfied. I was really stuck.

## The Battle with our Daughters

Sex wasn't the only thing that I had to struggle with. I had daughters now and I needed to be extra overprotective of them. I wouldn't let my husband change my oldest daughter diapers. First of all, she was the most beautiful little girl in the entire world. But my traumas made me believe that he would touch her, so I kept my eyes on him. I did this unknowingly. I wanted to believe that he was different but my life told me otherwise. I was bitter and angry. So, I watched my husband through those lenses. This wasn't fair to him nor me. We both had to suffer the consequences of my past.

My husband didn't know how to interact with our daughter because of the hurt goggles I was looking through. I was also loving my daughter through the lens of fear. We all know that there is no such thing as love and fear together. Perfect love casts down all fear. Fear and love cannot coexist. *1John4:18.*

I was loving my child though fear and tried to overcompensate by being in her presence at all times because I didn't want her to feel rejection. But what does a little 2-year old know about rejection?

Back then, I didn't have the language to articulate these moments. I had no idea that my traumas spilled on the people I loved the most. My husband, kids, friends whomever, should not have to bear this in the first place. My husband did not deserve this. He didn't do anything to me but I treated him in the response of those who did it to me. He had to be strong and he had to be led by something higher than his intellect. I'm telling you. The Lord was and is with him.

### How did My Husband Deal with Me?

My husband would have to keep adjusting and coming back with new ways to keep me. We began to worship more. We went into the wilderness together, a place of isolation where the Lord had to reign in our marriage. We couldn't do this on our own strength and ability. Once again, the kingdom had to show up and make our marriage stronger. Kingdom came so that we could be fortified. Our marriage would have to become the place where the Lord dwells. Our marriage would be the sacrifice where God could get the glory out of all of this.

Having children expedited my deliverance and walking through wholeness. I knew that what I was facing, my children couldn't face it. It wasn't their burden to bear. There was a great amount of selfishness from our previous generation to stay silent. We were taught to never bring shame upon the family and the family name because we have an image. Meanwhile, generational curses and patterns were getting stronger and stronger. The lies were told, dysfunction became the norm and little humans were sacrificed.

Perversion had a throne, and silence gave it a home. We didn't punish those who harmed us. Instead, we have family reunions that keep the innocent around the ones who hurt them. What type of safety was that?

Did we really think it would end with us? No, they found new meat, innocent targets to grab. We normalized this dysfunction and thought that change is supposed to happen. How could that be possible?

I'll tell you how my change began. It began with a made up mind and a trip to Georgia to tell the truth

# Chapter 15

## *"It Didn't Win"*

The moment I decided to tell my mom the truth was a day I'll never forget. What led me to that moment is just as important as how I got there. I began to embrace the changes that were happening to me. I began to outgrow certain phases in my life that also led me to outgrow certain people. If you couldn't grow with me, then you couldn't go with me. I could no longer be the planted pot, but the pot had to break the walls and its restrictions and be planted in a field.

I had to make some serious life adjustments to maintain the deliverance and healing that the Lord was taking me through. I remember my first deliverance session. I was being delivered from fear, death, and perversion. The response to perversion is one I could never forget. After deliverance, I had to stay away from certain atmosphere and environment that were in some of the people who I was attached to. That's because spirits know spirits. I'd say don't take it personal, it's spiritual.

I believe some of us are currently in relationships with individuals because we share the same spiritual battles. What we have in common is not limited to our experiences or traumas but spirits. Assess your environment. What are you around? You can be called to be the light in the dark places don't get me wrong, but you can also be in the wrong place for the season that God wants you in. Are you willing to give up your loyalty, which can become your stronghold, to be free? Are you willing to turn your back on your loved ones to be whole? Are you willing to give your friends to God so that you can find him for yourself?

Let me share with you a secret. A true friend will understand. They may feel some type of way but they will be alright. If you are here to better yourself, then they should be happy for you and be waiting for you on the other side. If you leave for better but they blame you, my darling let me set you free. Let them go. If it is meant to be, It will come back together.

A seed can hang around a bunch of seeds. You could live in the community filled with seeds. However, you will be limiting yourself to live around a bunch of "Should of, Could of, Would of's," and potential. A seed needs to break, it needs to crack, and it needs to fail. Start cracking around your friends and see what happens.

You have to go to a place where you can be buried in the right soil that can handle your brokenness. Deliverance breaks you! It's going to expose you, but let it be done in the dark as a seed does beneath the soil. You will be trampled upon and feel dirty. You will also be alone, no one will see you. It's okay, let your roots run deep. Let the Lord perform His marvelous work and allow the manifestation of his glory to emerge in due time.

An oak tree seed is small, but when it's planted in the right soil, in the right climate, in the right atmosphere, it will grow into a strong tree that will produce fruit that houses its seed. As a seed, you are powerful, but you are stronger when you fulfill the purposes that are inside of you.

I didn't want to go there but I feel that this is too important not to share. I had to stop caring about what others felt about me. I had to get delivered from people-pleasing and loyal because we were hanging out since grade school. I had to allow the Lord to surround me with the right community that will accept my brokenness. I had to find a community that will be the wise counsel that will help me grow.

I needed a trusted farmer to exercise wisdom, who won't reject me, but will be there to assist me. I needed the servant to notice the hands of the enemy, so that it would let the farmer know that there is something wrong. I needed the reaper at harvest time to extract the tares out of me, and take my wheat (fruit) into the storehouse or barn.

That's what happened when I went into the deep. No one was safe, not even myself. I had to let myself go, as well. I had to let go the thoughts of the world and my ways. I had to cast down my crown for the Lord. I had to distance myself from my mom. I didn't want to hurt her but I know that I did. I had to be free.

With this new mindset and many processes, I had to tell my mom what was going on with me. I realized that I tried to protect my parents' marriage at the cost of my sanity and I couldn't do it anymore. I didn't want to die. I didn't want my kids to endure this. I'm doing this because IT COULDN'T WIN! The devil couldn't win. I was fighting for way too long. It's my turn to walk in the best years of my life. A life in victory and power. The righteous Judge was about to strike

His hammer and declare me free.

# Chapter 16

*"The Beginning of wholeness"*

There were a few moments that aligned together that gave me the courage to travel to Georgia. It was literally a secret place experience that was being cultivated and music. My husband and I have a ministry known as AWAKE which is a prophetic worship culture. It stands for Authentic Worship And Kingdom Experience. The Lord birthed in us a platform of healing and deliverance through sounds and songs. We were hosting our fifth event "Strengthen Hearts," and we brought guests from out of town and from the local Hampton Roads area to participate.

During the event, The Lord was doing a marvelous work. Healing and deliverance were going forth when the worship leader at the time grabbed the microphone, asked for permission to speak and declared that this moment was a set up for us (My husband and I). She called the warriors aka intercessors with clean hands to come to our way and point as she prayed the fire from heaven. She began to pray and I broke. Everything that was happening in my private time with the Lord manifested.

I began to go through deliverance. Three worship warriors were there with me. My husband was there, an apostle was there, but most importantly God was there. This was the moment where I experienced the power of the Lord so strongly. I was being freed from so much bondage. The Lord cared about me so much that I was in a safe space to be opened up for surgery.

This was the moment of the harvesting of the wheat and the tare. I had to let my heart be opened to the Lord to make me clean. This was the moment I knew the Lord was setting the stage for me. This was the moment I've been waiting for!

**The Truth Will Set You Free**

It was finally the week to head to GA. I'm going to the hair show to turn up with my mother. I was going to give her the best time of her life. I wanted to make her smile because I knew when I told her the news, our lives will change forever. My husband and I left on a Friday night after my kids had gotten home from school. The goal was to pull up in GA in the wee hours of the morning like 2am-ish. That gave me a chance to rest and turn up all Saturday.

While we were driving, my husband had gotten really sick. I was too tired to drive but we weren't' far away from Raleigh. I called my homie and asked if we could stop by. She said yes and opened her doors. We were only supposed to be there until Sam got better. She told us she would keep us in prayer. I was numb. I was unsure. I was trying to stay as calm as possible.

We rose around 4am to head to GA. We still had about 5 hours to go to get to Atlanta. Throughout the trip, weird things occurred on the road. When my husband felt back to normal, my youngest son began to poop out of his clothing. We had to get off the exit to wash him up and change him. He had diarrhea and we were running low on pull-ups. We would wash him up, get a few miles down the road and it'll happen again.

As we traveled down I20, we were getting cut off by traffic. Cars were coming into our lane. As we pressed forward, we'd encounter a snow storm around exit 130. It began with hail and the clouds got really black. The snow came suddenly, the wind was strong, I was driving at the time so I had to slow down. As I navigated through the storm, a Jeep Cherokee flipped and we missed it. I prayed. Until we reached our exit. I felt safe again. We made it to the house and it's time to go.

My mom was happy to see us all again. I saw my auntie there and I was shocked that she brought my cousin with her. I was happy to see her because she's one of my favorites, no lie. I found her in the Jack and Jill bathroom connected to our rooms. She spoke to me, she randomly asked, "Von (my nickname), you bout to tell any? I'm like, tell huh? She proceeds to tell me about a dream that she had about me telling my mom and how it's been on her mind since she was coming down there. She was one of the few people who knew the truth.

Well, we get to the hair show and I promise you, I had the best time of my life. You'd think I was high or drunk because of how litty I was. On the way back, I gassed up my van so that we could pull out in the morning to head back to VA. When I left the gas station, my car powered down as I was getting onto the main road. I could have gotten hit but thankfully, there were no cars coming, so my mini van rolled across the street into a parking lot. My car refused to start at first. I looked at my cousin who shook her head. She and I knew what time it was. The van eventually started and we made it home.

My cousin remains in the car as we got our bags from all the shopping we did. She told me she's going to roll up a blunt because she was nervous. It was awkward at the house. I could feel this weird energy. I really can't explain what I felt but things felt off. I was watching in slow motion the smiles and the laughter from my family. I really had to enjoy this moment because I was freaking out.

The truth is I wanted to back down because the moment was too good to ruin. I didn't want to waste all of what I have gone through to get here and back down. I battled with timing. When would be the right time? Should I sit my parents down and tell them at the same time? I was trying to control the moment and let it happen the way it did in my head but I had too many realities to choose from. I would want it to be my mom, dad, me, and my husband present. The kids could be upstairs and my auntie could watch them. When I thought that was the winning plan, we'd get a phone call. A call that would change the trajectory of the night. My cousin who decided to stay back, took the car to the gas station and had gotten in a car accident by I20. She was terrified and wasn't making any sense. An instant panic came across us all. My aunt grabbed her things and my dad took her to the scene of the accident and they'd would be gone for hours.

I went upstairs defeated. My mom was cleaning her house and informing the family members back in South Carolina on what was going on. I called my friend via FaceTime, only to begin having an anxiety attack. I began to shake, I couldn't breath, and I was fading away. My husband was right there praying for peace and declaring my sanity. I was losing it! My friend began to war with us as well. When I came back to "normal," I took a deep breath and told them now is the time. I told Sam to stay in the room.

It was going on 12am and my mom was at the beginning of the stairwell sweeping. I said momma, I have to talk to you. She said about what. I'm like, "I don't know how to say it." She said, "Von, just say it."

In one deep breath I said, mama, I've been molested by daddy from the ages around ten to fifteen years old. My mom said WHAAAT??!!! Omg, VON, why didn't you tell me?! I told her I was too afraid. My mom would then move from the stairs to her island to take a seat. It was really thick. She said, "Von, tell me what happened. I'm stronger than you think." She made the environment easy to talk to. It was like I was talking to a really cool friend.

For the very first time in life I told her everything. I told her when it happened. How it happened. Not many details but I shared with her every encounter that ever happened. EVERYTHING! I decided if I'm going to rip her heart open, let me do it all in one motion so that I don't keep reopening the wounds. My mom would listen and ask very little questions. She also shared intimate moments about her life.

When all was said and done, my mom apologized to me. She confessed that she didn't have any idea. However, if she would have known she would have gotten me out a long time ago. I told her about my uncertainty. I confessed that I was afraid to talk to her and how I've been fighting for a while now, but I was tired of holding it in.

We shared so much with one another that night. Her final words to me were, "I'm sorry you had to hold this in for so long. I want you to go upstairs and rest well. I want you to sleep well tonight. I'll handle this when he gets home. I won't yell, nor scream, I'm going to pray and ask the Lord to give me the words to say because he has been preparing me for the past few weeks with dreams." I said goodnight, I love you.

The keys opened the mudroom door. My father and auntie were coming back. My parents went upstairs. I spoke with my aunt for a little bit about my cousin and I went to bed. During pillow talk, I told my husband what happened. He said he was proud of me. He gave me a hug and we went to sleep briefly.

I was awakened by a text from my mom that my dad wanted to speak with me. I didn't see this far. I didn't think about speaking to him but it was something that I dreamed about. I always wondered what the moment would be like and I was about to find out. I came downstairs and my father was at the island sitting down holding his head. He was at a loss for words. He was sweating. He was hurt, angry, and sweating. It was bad.

When my Father opened his mouth to speak to me, I felt like I was talking to a young boy. He mustered up the strength to tell me that he apologizes and asks me to forgive him. He began to confess some things as well. I was listening as my father began to speak from his heart. When he spoke, I could feel the torment in his mind. I didn't want to see him like this. I didn't like it and it hurt me to see my father hurting.

When I was able to speak, I told my father that I waited for this moment my entire life. I fantasized about it for years wondering if I would embrace him? Everything I imagined was false. It didn't happen like the movies. It didn't play out like I assumed it would. The real truth was there was a feeling of love that overtook me. All I could feel was love and great compassion. I wanted to embrace him but I sat there watching him. I told my father that I had already forgiven him. I had to so that I can be free, but to hear it further tells me that I am. I began to thank him and I solidified it with I forgive you. I told I'm that I loved him. He kept apologizing and I'm like, "It's cool pops."

# The Start of Something New

It was time to hit the road. We got the kids up, my aunt was downstairs making breakfast, while we were figuring out how to get my cousin out of jail. Yes, my cousin who was involved in the car accident the night before, went to jail after leaving the hospital due to warrants. As we packed, I saw a text my father sent of him wanting both my husband and I to pray for him. It was a shock but we were ready. We let the kids go downstairs with my auntie and we went into my parent's room.

I don't remember much of the dialogue but I do remember the position. My mom was far away from my dad. My husband was already in the room with my father. My dad's posture emitted the emotions of hurt, shame, and disappointment. I can't imagine what was running through his mind. I know we began in prayer. My husband began by allowing God to enter into this place, we began with repenting and for the next few hours, we were in the posture of deliverance.

During that moment, I witnessed the true love of God. I witnessed the strength of the strongholds as well. I knew God was greater. I saw the torment that was over my father. We heard spirits of crying out. We felt the struggle of oppression. It wasn't all my fathers fault. I learned so much about spiritual oppression and how LOVE conquers all. Real LOVE! As we prayed for my dad, my mom would come over and lay her hands on him to pray for him. The room was filled with the presence of God. It was his glory and we saw it working. This was just the beginning.

When we left, I felt as light as a feather. I felt like I could ascend and touch God's lips. I felt like the angels were with me. I felt free from the very first time. However, I left a big pile of dog poop for my parents to go through.

This was the beginning of their wholeness. This moment was to kick start seeking the Lord like never before. I can't control what happens there but for the next moments of my life, I had to learn that wholeness isn't a magical thing. Wholeness is something that I am currently walking through. This book is being written 5 months after telling my parents the news. Writing this book has been therapy and has brought a new level of deliverance as I type and converse with my husband about these moments.

Since then, I've been seeking the Lord like never before. I've been asking the Lord to search my heart. I prayed that the Lord would place me in great company. I wanted to be surrounded by kingdom and wise counsel in it. I prayed and God revealed to me that He will restore my years.

I'm finally living. I will look like the future of what God has called for me and that's to prosper and be in good health. Not just a physical health, but mental, emotional, and spiritual. Now, let me begin to wrap all of this up because honestly this story is being written daily.

# Chapter 17

Over the next few months, so much took place. In February I told my mom's parents my big news. In March, The Corona Virus made it to the US and quarantine began. My kids were out of school and we were going back to Georgia. We felt it would be a great opportunity to talk and mend. We knew that they were faced with a serious challenge, but we were willing to do whatever it took to create a new norm. Being in Georgia was challenging. I was consumed with work and school. While I was there, I was finishing up my final two classes of grad school and cultivating new relationships.

My mom wanted my attention and I wasn't giving her the attention she desired. Corona was still in its new phases, so all of Georgia was shut down. We were forced to stay in the house and we couldn't run from the huge elephant. It was always there and we wouldn't touch it. We avoided it. We didn't discuss the situation and I wasn't at peace.

Tensions were rising. I would find myself getting upset because my mom wanted things a certain type of way. She's a clean person who loves order and she suffers from OCD. I have four kids so, maintaining the excellent standard in my mom's house was hard. Maintaining silence started to get challenging. The decibels had to be at a minimum. There were rules in my mom house that I didn't want to follow. I didn't feel it was realistic.

There were two households under one roof, with two different mindsets, and multiple children that were filled with energy, causing everyone to have to change and make adjustments. I was insensitive because at the time I was only thinking about me and my household. There was a deeper issue I was experiencing. I could feel the pain of my mom's heart from the thing that I told her a few weeks prior. However, I wasn't sensitive to her coping style. I was in a process and became free. Yet, my freedom placed my mom in a new process. I wasn't the same daughter February ago. How was she to deal with her husband? Truth is, her life actually changed.

I remember talking to my father who expressed my mom's heart but I wanted her to tell me, not him. I disagreed with a lot of things that were said. I wanted my parents to understand that I was going to do what makes me happy. I was not to blame because I'm choosing happiness.

Things got worse. My husband and I key-board amp went out and we were unable to worship in the house with our keyboard. I had my guitar so we tried to do something with that but the keys were vital to my husband. Once the amp went out, things changed even more. My husband started picking up on the spiritual activity and he warned me not to take anything personally because we wrestle not against flesh and blood. He told me to be patient.

The breaking point for me was driving to Savannah to get some seafood. My friend called and my mom exploded. She screamed and showed an emotion that I've never seen before. Things got weird. She wouldn't talk to me, she ignored me. Once again, I didn't understand at the time why she would get so upset.

We'd converse but it was small talk. We wouldn't address the elephant in the room. As I write, my heart aches because my mom was battling her own war and needed to go through her own deliverance. I had to chill, I had to learn how to navigate now. I don't want to upset my mom, but I wasn't about to be controlled either. All I wanted was to obtain my freedom.

I saw myself shrinking back into the 12-year-old girl that I used to be that could take orders and never complain. My mom wanted things to go back to normal. But I wasn't complying to those standards. I no longer wanted to be treated like a child but an adult. Let's talk. I tried to flex my undergrad degree in psychology to get information because she wasn't talking. It only made matters worse.

My dad, on the other hand, was around. From the outside looking in, he was chilling living his best life. He didn't seem to be punished. My father was back to his day to day life, riding motorcycles, watching his ghost stories, talking to Sam, and playing with my children. It didn't seem like anything was wrong. We'd chat a bit from time to time but I remember going out to speak with him intentionally. We were out on the front porch where he revealed that I was at their house for about a month, and that moment was the first time that I took the time to talk to him. Honestly, I wanted to avoid him. I didn't have much to say. It was tough trying to navigate and I had to be led, not my emotions, but with love. However, We had a really good conversation that day.

I would make small gestures come into his world. I'd take trips with my mom and dad to the store, we'd go and get ice cream and I'll help him with yard work. I also had the chance to ride on the back of the motorcycle with him. I learned he was dealing with this issue in his own way. He took long bike rides to clear his mind. He was riding to deal with whatever it is that he dealt with. He apologizes even more. I had to assure him that it's all good, just let God be God. I'm okay.

It was really challenging for me to be in my parent's home for six weeks. While I was there, I began to work out again. I also went back into my secret place which was my dad's closet in my room. I went back into the posture of prayer.

I remember praying to be freed from control. During that prayer, the Lord began to show me, me.

The Lord had to reveal to me my toxic ways before praying about someone else's fault.

I went through deliverance in the closet that day. This was the first time I placed my hands on myself to do so. All I wanted was to be happy and whole. I was tired at this point, tired of being in the position I was in. I was tired of being a do-girl and a people-pleaser. I was also tired of fighting and taking things personally.

Me choosing my happiness had to be intentional because I never did anything for myself. I would make choices according to what others would think. Therefore, I never got what I wanted. I did according to what I thought others wanted.

2020 was the beginning of the entire world changing. It may seem like this is the worst year in history but this is the best year for me. This is the year that I realize that I am enough. I won't get it right but I will be whole. I will choose the kingdom every single time. If God says it, then I trust that all things will work together for the good of those who love Him.

## Walking in Kingdom

I felt it was selfish that my parents didn't understand that all of this was a part of my healing. I didn't understand that I needed to change my expectations because they were not realistic. How could I expect my parents, who were still trying to navigate their new norm, to understand where I am? I was walking in offense of my journey to wholeness. That's because my wholeness was shallow. I would find out that deliverance is just an introduction to wholeness.

When you are walking in wholeness, you have to understand that it's a process that you have to take step-by-step. It's literally following the footprints of the One who has gone before you. The steps of Christ have caused me to walk on water through faith but really go into the deep.

The truth of the matter is, when you begin to walk in the kingdom, the ways of the world will not understand until they adopt true kingdom principles. These principles are not some 12-step journey to wholeness that we can follow along with. Your journey will be different. That's because everyone has a different position in the kingdom. When you were created, you were designed to be unique. The same experiences the enemy tried to use to kill you, the tares that were sown, was only the power of the Glory of God to be revealed in your life.

Your testimony is the beginning of a revealing kingdom. This is the wheat that will be taken into the barn or the storehouse to give to those who are in need. Come on fruit!!! This is why deliverance is so important to those who are believers or who want to believe. It is the gathering of the tares and the wheat. It is the beginning of a new life that the Lord has for you. This new life is the real life that you have yet to experience.

True deliverance begins when you begin to confront your pains and trauma. Confront those things that hurt you and begin to confess it. Give it all to God, because he knows. He understands. He has been waiting for you to get to this point with his arms out-stretched.

## My Near-Death Experience

I remember a dream I had where Satan grabbed me. I had this dream about a month before writing this book. Satan grabbed me and told me he was going to kill me. I was in his arms and could see the clever shape shifter that was trying to scare me. I wasn't afraid. I declared that I will live and not die. You can not kill me.

I was ascending high in the atmosphere. I was thinking he was going to drop me but I knew that if that happened the Lord would capture me. I kept going higher and higher. Then, I started seeing a bright light. When I saw the light, I panicked. I was going to die! This bright white light was so intense that I had to turn my back towards it. When I got close to the light, Satan told me that I will die because surely, no man should see God and live! With my back turned, I closed my eyes tightly and asked God to forgive me. I want to live. The Lord took me out of Satan's grasp and placed me on a rock. On this rock, I saw a moving green stream, and I jumped in and dropped down into Glory. I heard sounds that I've never heard before. I also felt the Lord fighting Satan on my behalf up top while I'm in the middle of somewhere.

When I woke up, the Lord spoke to me and revealed that the enemy did exactly what he was supposed to do. Push you into my presence! This is how God gets the glory and I want you to pay attention. What was meant for you bad ,the Lord will turn it around for His good. Remember, God created all things and said that it was good except for man to be alone.

I was never alone. Even in my torment, I was never alone. At the age of five, I was never alone. When I was going through all of the things I went through, the Lord was there. He kept me through it all. Many people would not survive walking in my shoes. I've heard of those who have been admitted into the mental institution because of this type of pain. I've read about those who have committed suicide because of this pain. I've seen many turn away from God completely because of this type of experience. I could have been strung out on drugs so I can stay in my alternate realities. I wasn't supposed to be here. I kept crying out, I kept fighting, and at the right time I'm able to share this experience with you.

## Choose Deliverance

Deliverance began with confronting my past. I had to face my fears. I also had to confess to the Lord, I'm not well and I need your help. I tried everything in my own strength but I lacked joy. I found that the joy of the Lord, the happiness and completeness of God is His joy, which gives me strength. I had to release those toxic ways in me. I had to release those who I had given rule over me. I had to release the pain and weight by taking on the yoke of God because His yoke is easy and his burdens are light. Confront. Confess. Release. This isn't a three step guide to deliverance, this is just three things that I had to do to begin my process to walk in wholeness.

Wholeness once again, is an every day, step-by-step, type of thing. It's not a race, you go at your pace. Stay focused and don't look back. The only thing waiting for you is familiarity. What's ahead of you is your future and purpose. What's ahead of you is your manifestation of fruit. What's ahead of you is who the Lord knew before he formed you in your mother's womb. I refuse to leave this earth while doing enough to stay saved. I will not live a life below the standard that God has for me. I've suffered in poverty long enough. I don't care what riches and wealth I obtain, if it's not in Jesus's name, if it doesn't bring glory to God, then, I DON'T WANT IT! No wealth of the land I can take. Gold, money, houses, cars, all of that belongs to God anyways. What belongs to me is the wealth of the kingdom, the promise of everlasting life.

I realized that earth is a temporary place. I now understand that my traumas brought pain to my flesh, but as the body heals itself, it took God to heal my heart and mind. Not the organ and muscle, but the supernatural place where He dwells.

# Chapter 18

*A book that's still being written…*

Now that you have read my story, let me share with you all, that I'm still in this process and I'll forever be in a process as long as I'm breathing. I had to learn how to trust God, and I had to become open to deliverance. Churches may have deliverance or kingdom in their names, but it's not in the name alone that qualifies one to deliver. It is the heart, relationship, and intentions with God that gives you the permission.

You have permission when you walk with him and get to know him. I'm not calling you to become a demon buster. This is not a joke nor a game. This isn't something to be taken lightly. My experience leads me to connect with the right community and ministry that will help me mature and grow in this gifting that the Lord has placed in me. A place of deliverance and transformation for real!

I ask that you allow the Lord to search your heart. If you are in need of deliverance, I pray that the Lord will send someone your way. I pray that you'll have an open and repentant heart to receive Him. I pray that he will surround you with the right community with wise counsel. Remember, all things that were made were good EXCEPT for man to be alone. You can not live in this world by yourself in isolation. That's the place the enemy wants you to be. He understands the power or community and the power of accountability.

Before, I've never seen the power of God go beyond emotionalism and feel good stuff. The times that deliverance occurred in the churches of my past, I remember the children having to leave because spirits could jump into the weakest vessels. This is true, but spirits are not only jumping during expelling, but through silence and not telling, or through fear that prevents you from not sharing the power that is in your story.

I wanted to title this last chapter the juicy journey to wholeness or the confessions of resentment, bitterness, hate, and unforgiveness. Truth is, "This a book that is still being written," is perfect because every day I have to choose to fight for wholeness. I have to lay down my will and flesh to choose the will of the Father. I don't want to be lukewarm but I want to align with the person I was before I came into the womb of my mother.

This can only happen by deliverance which is simply love. For God so loved the world that he gave his only begotten son… John 3:16 but do we know what that means? In the next few paragraphs, I'm going to share with you my journey to deliverance. It didn't come through my bachelor's degree in Psychology from a known Christian university, but it came from being in the presence of the Lord and in the right place with the right people at the right time (community).

Truth is, I couldn't have gotten to this place by myself. I needed to align my heart to be yielded towards my Father. I am learning that as long as I'm breathing, I have a purpose. If I have a purpose, then there is a promise attached to it. That promise is my blueprint, the word that was spoken over my life. In order to get to the promise, I have to be processed. It's the process that takes me to my next place. Processes are kinetic. It's the wind to take you where you need to go.

I needed a new approach. A different perspective. I had to follow the Truth. The reality of my childhood up to this present moment was meant to destroy me but it took me to a place where I am confident in who I am. My past does not define me but it did make me.

I'm also learning that my healing wasn't in anything tangible. I once used people to fill the potholes in my heart, but I needed wholeness to come forth to begin to build healthy relationships. My healing didn't come from Holy Oil that was placed on my head in the shape of a cross. It wasn't in a title or position. I had to try God and have faith that it is so. I had to remove pride. I had to humble myself. I needed to confess that I was broken and sick.

I understand that the giftings of God come without repentance but when I was feeling alone in my isolation, the Lord would creatively reveal Himself to me. Through my pain and my processes he'd reveal my heart. In my dreams and through his Word. The bible though it is tangible is also a spirit that wakes up when you allow it to come alive in you. I had to be okay with being alone. I had to own the rejection that came with change in me. My willingness to pursue a relationship with God was important. My husband couldn't have done this had I not be ready to receive the love of God and experience deliverance.

For me, deliverance came by the confession of what it was I was being delivered from. I had to confess that I was bitter, that I did resent my family and those who hurt me. I was bitter that no man could love me to the desired intimacy I wanted. I was bitter because I felt like my mom didn't see me because she was in church, powerful, and anointed. I was bitter with my father for lying. He lied so well. He lied because he never told my mom the truth. I didn't think my mom should find out from me at the age of 29. My dad could have been man enough to tell her. But I was also a liar because It took me 20 years to confess the truth.

I was bitter that I loved him but hated what he's done to me at the same time. I could never be angry with my brother. I'm sure he has his own story to tell but he was only doing what he saw or what was passed down and not dealt with. I was bitter because I thought God left me too.

I had to confess unforgiveness. I learned how to forgive others but I didn't forgive myself. I blamed myself because I let what happened to me happen for so long. All I had to do was tell the moment it happened. But there were so many damaging reasons why I couldn't. My mom loves my father so much and he's a provider, but I felt like she would have been crippled if she left. I felt that if she remarried, her man could do this to me. I felt there was no way to avoid this. Honestly, this was control showing up again. I tried to make the best decision made from the broken places of my reality.

What wasn't confessed by my mouth had to be confessed with an open heart. When the Lord started sending his prophets my way, I had to trust the word of God from their lips. When I had to undergo my first deliverance it was through FaceTime with an artist which kickstarted this whole thing. I had to be delivered from bitterness and unforgiveness, she gave me references to read and I was on it. I started learning about pride and how to detect the spirits that you speak to and how to pray and move in deliverance. The more I read the more open I became.

My next deliverance session would happen after I left my aunt's funeral to come back home. I had a chance to speak some remarks, but it went to a different place. I saw the cloud of the Lord in that space. I was speaking in front of my family and the Lord showed up and out. My family was touched by God, but I returned home afflicted with three spirits. This was my first time experiencing the manifestations of them. I learned through that moment that's when deliverance and healing were activated in me and my husband.

I would soon find out that there were things that lie dormant like lust. That the seeds that weren't expelled would be long dormant waiting to erupt. I also had to stop living in denial. I was saying to myself before the writing of this book that my past wasn't that bad. I would say to myself that it was simply this or that and I tried to downplay it. Truth be told it was worse. I couldn't fit everything in this book but as I write, I see old memories that I had to deal with.

The Bible tells us in Matthew 12:28, *"but if I cast out demons by the spirit of God, surely the kingdom of God has come upon you."* This is Jesus speaking. The kingdom of God shows up and demons tremble and flee. Jesus spoke of deliverance.

We have to be honest with ourselves. As I write this book, my marriage, myself included, has experienced even more deliverance. My husband and I had to confess lust. I had to confess the stories of me victimizing my cousin. I had to ask God to remind me of other moments that I may have forgotten about. A great friend of mine would tell me that deliverance requires maintenance. Just because you are delivered doesn't mean trials and testing wouldn't come your way. Every new height and every deeper depth in God, every new journey will bring a new level of deliverance, even from old things. This is why confronting and confessing. This is the beginning of the exposure. Walk in truth, walk in the Light. Tell your story at the right place and time.

Wholeness is not a one-time guarantee. Every day, I must` walk. I must choose to stay in the presence of God. I learned that my desire for intimacy only reflects his purpose for me. He desires that I give him his time. Therefore, the enemy perverted intimacy so I wouldn't get to this point, and to know where and who I am. I say this with confidence that I've made it to the place that the devil didn't want me to be. I was supposed to be dead, I'm not supposed to be in my right mind. But God rescued me and continues to rescue me time after time. He'll do it for you too. This is my story. It's still being written.

# *Prayer*

*I pray that my story touches you in a way to help to see differently. I hope that you all take the necessary measures in your walk of wholeness and that you will be seen and handled properly. I pray that you connect to living water. I pray that if counseling is what you need, you turn to the wonderful counselor who will teach you all things but also get the much help that you need. I pray that even now chains will begin to break, and scales will be removed from your eyes. I pray that you experience a renewed mind and heart in Jesus name.*

*I am calling upon you oh Father, to rest in the hearts of those who have read this book. I pray that deliverance shall spring forth. I pray that healing shall manifest, that your seeds will blossom into your purposed fruit. And even now oh God, I come against any enemy that will try to steal the seeds of life that are planted in this book. I pray that it shall fall on good ground* and multiplied 30, 60, 100-fold oh God. I pray that people will become awakened to their spiritual oppression and be loosed in Jesus name.

I call upon you oh God to rest in every word in this book. That every word will have your healing and transformative power. That when the person reading this makes it to the final period, they would have encountered your love, your presence, surrender their faults, create an altar to burn away the tares, and be healed and be whole. I pray that the tough conversations will be had, and that shame will not come upon their family but fame in your name Father that you will be glorified. Father God, I pray that lives will be changed, families will be mended with the glory of you oh Lord.

I pray that this book starts the beginning of a movement that will move true. I pray now, that the generational curse stops here. That we will be the vessels to end this. I pray that faith arises even now. That your sons and daughters will run back to you. That your arms are extended to receive them with your loving-kindness. I pray that the people experience your fruit. That they identify their roots and that you will do the harvesting in due time. I pray that your servants will see again oh God. That they will see the tares in other lives, including their own. I pray that those who battle with control be freed from the bands of witch-craft. In the name of Jesus.

I pray that identities will be found through this book but ultimately in You. I pray for everyone reading, Father, that they will be saved and accept you as your Lord and Savior. I pray that Your water of glory crashes upon them even now. That the Holy Spirit will enter. That they will speak in a heavenly lan-guage. That the presence of God overtakes them and they are not afraid. I pray that You will be pleased with your sons and daugh-ters. I pray that his book will bring forth new marriages, healthy *marriages, that will bring glory unto you oh Father. I pray that*

*your church comes home. That your orphans return to you oh*

*God. I pray that you have your way in each and every one of our*

*lives. In your son Jesus name, we pray. Amen.*

# About the Author

Tre'elle was born and raised in Beaufort, South Carolina and has journeyed across the seas as a former Navy Sailor. She has her Bachelors in Psychology from Regent University and a Masters in Digital Audience Strategies from Arizona State University.

She is the founder of Tag It Brand It, a digital marketing and branding company. She's also the co-founder AWAKE Worship, a platform for Authentic Worship And Kingdom Experience, Couple Convo, a place for married couples and those who are looking to get married one day, and Vision PINK, and organization for women to pursue their Purpose IN Kingdom.

Tre'elle is an artist and poet. She's released an EP "Unspoken Words" which is poetry and two singles Genesis and Heaven Invade. She loves the Most High God with all of her heart. She understands that she has a powerful story and wants to share it with the world. Her desires are for all things that she releases in the Earth to align with Isaiah 61:1-3.

She lives in Hampton Roads, VA with her husband and four children.

Made in the USA
Columbia, SC
29 March 2021